THE ETERNAL RELIGION

THE ETERNAL RELIGION

Glimpses of Hinduism

Karan Singh

SPEAKING TIGER

SPEAKING TIGER BOOKS LLP
125-A, Ground Floor, Shahpur Jat
New Delhi—110049

First published by Speaking Tiger Books, 2023

ISBN: 978-93-5447-665-5
eISBN: 978-93-5447-666-2

10 9 8 7 6 5 4 3 2 1

Typeset in Adobe Garamond Pro by SÜRYA, New Delhi
Printed at Chaman Enterprises, New Delhi

As flowing rivers, from wheresoever they may arise, merge into the same ocean casting off name and form, so do the knowers, from wheresoever they may come, attain to the same Supreme Divinity, freed from all limitations.

—*Mundaka Upanishad*

CONTENTS

PART FOUR: Selections from Hindu Texts and Seers

PREFACE

The Essence of Hinduism

I have been writing on a variety of subjects, but mainly on Hinduism and spirituality, for seventy years now, since 1953, when I was 22 years old. Many of my essays and articles have been published in various journals and anthologies over the decades, and quite a few have been collected and issued in book form. However, several longer and perhaps more thoughtful essays are now unavailable. My publisher Ravi Singh from Speaking Tiger suggested that a collection of these longer reflections on Hinduism, including some pieces on my travels to places of pilgrimage, would be of interest to serious students of what is perhaps the world's most ancient living religion. It is with this in mind that this book is being published. It is my tribute to a religion that I believe to be one of humanity's most evolved and sophisticated spiritual traditions.

There have been some highly unfortunate and derogatory comments made recently about Sanatana Dharma. This term, which means 'the eternal religion', is virtually interchangeable with 'Hinduism', and dates far back into the past. Even the Buddha ends one of his sermons with the words *'Essa Dharma Sanatana'*. The context for the troubling comments against Sanatana Dharma, or Hinduism, is the practice of untouchability. This abominable practice has no place whatsoever in a free, egalitarian society—indeed, in any society that would claim to be civilized—and it has been rightly condemned by every Hindu social reformer, from Raja Rammohun Roy and Jyotiba Phule to Swami Vivekananda and Mahatma Gandhi. It is banned in the Indian Constitution and despite a tremendous backlog of oppression, the situation is gradually improving. Of course, much more needs to be done to root this poison out of Hindu society. But to look upon untouchability as the central feature of the Hindu ethos would be as distorted as to look upon the inquisition and witch-hunting as the central features of the Christian ethos.

It is true, and perhaps inevitable, that in the five thousand years or more of its history, a number of undesirable and objectionable practices have sought shelter under the vast umbrella of the Hindu faith. After all, when literally billions of people have professed a certain religion through several thousand years, the weaknesses of different social and economic structures will necessarily be reflected in various quasi-religious customs and rituals. However, it will be unfair to ascribe all these ills to Hinduism. In fact, looked at from the reverse angle, it can be claimed that the credit for maintaining the cohesion of such a vast mass of humanity for so long a period, and for producing a major civilization with some of the greatest achievements of art, culture, and philosophy known to man, can largely be traced to the deep influence of Hinduism upon the Indian people.

There are, as I see it, four fundamental concepts that are at the core of Hinduism, rather than the vast mass of ritual and often crass superstition that has grown around it over the millennia. These concepts, which I discuss in detail in three different essays included in this volume, are contained in the majestic Upanishads. They are:

(a) The entire cosmos is a spiritual emanation, sprung from the divine, pervaded by the divine and yet not in any way limiting the fullness of divine plenitude.
(b) There is within each human being, irrespective of caste or creed, race or gender, religion or nationality, a spark of the divine consciousness, whereby all humans are 'children of immortality'.
(c) The divine within (the microcosm) and the Divine without (the macrocosm) are in fact the same.
(d) The highest destiny and goal of man is to unite his limited individual consciousness with the vast ocean of divinity that pervades the universe.

The theory of karma could, perhaps, be added to the list as a fifth concept.

The aberrations of caste or the abominations of untouchability do not really touch this central core of Hinduism. Whatever may or may not be the distorted conception of some people, the Hindu ethos teaches a spiritual equality and a universalism that has no parallel.

I have no desire to gloss over the tremendous social and personal disabilities that various aspects of Hindu customs have imposed through the centuries. However, living as we now are in a free nation based on the principles of justice, liberty, equality and fraternity, we must continue to shed the inessential encrustations that had gathered around the central core of this great religion over the last many centuries. It is my belief that Hinduism has, and will continue to have for as long as humanity exists, the power to provide inspiration and illumination to many millions throughout the world, whether or not they formally belong to the Hindu faith. This volume is the result of that lifelong belief.

KARAN SINGH
November 2023

PART ONE

Hinduism: An Overview

The religion that has come to be known as Hinduism is certainly the oldest and most varied of all the great religions of the world. The word 'Hinduism' itself is a geographical term based upon the Sanskrit name for the great river, known as the Sindhu, that runs across the northern boundaries of India. For those living on the other side of this river, the entire region to the southeast of the Sindhu, which the Greeks called the Indus, came to be known as the land of the Hindus, and the vast spectrum of faiths that flourished here acquired the generic name Hinduism. In fact, Hinduism calls itself the Sanatana Dharma, the eternal faith, because it is based not upon the teachings of a single preceptor but on the collective wisdom and inspiration of great seers and sages from the very dawn of Indian civilisation—perhaps the oldest living civilisation of the world.

The Scriptures

The Sanskrit word for philosophy is *darshana* or 'seeing', which implies that Hinduism is not based merely on intellectual speculation but is grounded upon direct and immediate perception. This, in fact, distinguishes Indian philosophy from much of Western philosophical thought. The oldest and most important scriptures of Hinduism are the Vedas, which contain inspired utterances of seers and sages who had achieved a direct perception of the divine being. The Vedas are considered to be eternal, because they are not merely superb poetic compositions but represent the divine truth itself as perceived through the elevated consciousness of great seers. The four Vedas—the Rig, the Yajur, the Sama and the Atharva—contain between them over a hundred thousand verses, which include some of the greatest mystical poetry ever written. For example, the famous 'Hymn of Creation' in the Rig Veda is an extraordinary utterance. It has been translated by Ralph T.H. Griffith as follows:

Then was not non-existent nor existent:
there was no realm of air, no sky beyond it.
What covered in, and where? And what gave shelter?
Was water there, unfathomed depth of water?

Death was not then, nor was there aught immortal:
No sign was there, the day's and night's divider.
That One thing, breathless, breathed by its own nature:
apart from it was nothing whatsoever.

Darkness there was: at first concealed in darkness
this All was indiscriminated chaos.
All that existed then was void and formless:
by the great power of Warmth was born that Unit.

Thereafter rose Desire in the beginning,
Desire, the primal seed and germ of Spirit.
Sages who searched with their hearts' thought discovered
the existent's kinship in the non-existent.

Transversely was their severing line extended:
what was above it then, and what below it?
There were begetters, there were mighty forces,
free action here and energy up yonder.

Who verily knows and who can here declare it,
whence it was born and whence comes this creation?
The Gods are later than this world's production.
Who knows then whence it first came into being?

He, the first origin of this creation,
whether he formed it all or did not form it,
whose eye controls this world in highest heaven,
he verily knows it, or perhaps he knows not.

The Vedas contain beautiful hymns addressed to various powers of nature such as the Sun, the Moon, the Ocean, the Rain, the Dawn—all pervaded by a deep intuitive awareness of the essential unity and interconnectedness behind these phenomena. Portions deal with the ritual worship of the early Aryans, the *yajna* sacrifice revolving around the sacred fire which was looked upon as the intermediary between the human and the divine powers. There is also a fascinating array of medical prescriptions, especially in the Atharva Veda, and a great deal of other social material including hymns to matrimony and friendship, prayers for progeny, longevity, cattle, and prosperity. Taken together, they constitute a unique document of the religious consciousness of all humanity. It is virtually a miracle that they came down intact through thousands of years entirely by memory, a fantastic feat of mnemonics for which countless generations of seers deserve unqualified gratitude. It was only in the middle of the 19th century that the great orientalist, Friedrich Max Müller, brought out the first printed edition of the Rig Veda.

The Upanishads are known as the Vedanta, or the end of the Vedas, both because they come at the end of the Vedic collections and also because they represent the culmination of Vedic teachings. One hundred and eight Upanishads have been preserved, of which at least fourteen are of major importance. These remarkable dialogues between the teacher and one or more pupils deal with the deepest problems of human existence, of death and other realms of being, of the goal of life, and the stages of spiritual realisation. The *Isha Upanishad*, though containing only eighteen verses, is considered to be probably the most important such text. Its famous first line, 'This entire cosmos, whatever is still or moving, is pervaded by the divine', contains the very essence of Hinduism.

The *Mundaka Upanishad* has a beautiful verse which brings out the essential role of the Upanishads as vehicles for spiritual realisations:

> *Having taken as a bow the great weapon of the Upanishads, one should fix on it the arrow sharpened by constant meditation; drawing it with a mind filled with That (Brahman*), penetrate, O handsome youth, the Imperishable as the target.*

---

*The unchanging, permanent, highest reality; the all-pervasive, infinite, eternal truth; that which causes all that is, that which is all that is.

The *Katha Upanishad* contains the memorable dialogue between the boy Nachiketa and Yama, the god of Death, and represents a remarkable formulation of the Vedantic gospel. It is significant that in Hinduism death is not something to be looked upon with horror and hatred, but is rather considered to be as essential an aspect of existence as life, part of the inescapable dualities of day and night, heat and cold, good and evil, joy and sorrow that are woven into the very texture of manifested existence. It is only by transcending these dualities and attaining the *brahmasthiti*, the state of Brahman, that the human being can finally fulfil his cosmic destiny.

Contrary to a popular misconception often encountered in the West, Hinduism is not a passive, world-negating religion. It is a vibrant, life-affirming faith, using 'life' in the deeper sense of that supreme poise that transcends the dualities of life and death. According to the Hindu view, there is a supreme state into which it is possible for the human consciousness to enter and which, once achieved, places one above the endless cycle of rebirth in which the entire cosmos is imprisoned. The sage Shvetashvatara says in the great Upanishad that bears his name: 'I know that Great Being, effulgent like the Sun shining on the other shore beyond the darkness.' And Lord Krishna also describes (in the Bhagavad Gita) the supreme goal as 'the light of lights beyond the darkness'.

The attainment of this exalted state of consciousness is not incompatible with action in this world. While it is true that there has always been a significant stand of renunciation in Hinduism, which found fuller expression in the Jain and Buddhist traditions that flowed from the mother faith, it is useful to remember that the goal of Hinduism is a luminous, glowing state of supreme bliss, not a negative self-annihilation.

There are five basic tenets that underlie Hinduism which, if properly understood, provide the key to an understanding of a faith that is bewildering in its apparent diversity and complexity.

The first is the concept of Brahman, the unchanging, undying reality that pervades the entire cosmos. The Vedic seers saw that everything in the universe changes, and they called the creation *samsara*, that which always moves. But they also perceived that behind this change there was an unchanging substratum from which the changing worlds emanated like sparks from a great fire. This supreme, all-pervasive entity known as Brahman has been beautifully described in various Upanishads. Thus, the *Mundaka Upanishad* has the following verse:

Brahman verily is this immortal being.
In front is Brahman, behind is Brahman.
To the right and to the left.
It spreads forth above and below.
Verily, Brahman is this effulgent universe.

Similarly, the following important passage in the *Shvetashvatara Upanishad* shows clearly that although the Hindus worshipped many manifestations of the divine, they realised that behind them all there was the same all-pervasive Brahman:

Thou art the fire,
Thou art the sun,
Thou art the air,
Thou art the moon,
Thou art the starry firmament,
Thou art Brahman Supreme:
Thou art the waters—Thou
The creator of all!

Thou art woman,
thou art man,
Thou art the youth,
thou art the maiden,
Thou art the old man tottering with his staff;
Thou are the faces everywhere.
Thou art the dark butterfly,
Thou art the green parrot with red eyes,
Thou art the thunder cloud, the seasons, the seas.
Without beginning art thou.
Beyond time, beyond space,
Thou art he from whom sprang
The three worlds.

Filled with Brahman are the things we see;
Filled with Brahman floweth all that is; From Brahman
all—yet is he still the same.

The second great insight of the Vedic seers was that, as the changing universe outside was pervaded by the Brahman, the changing world within man himself was based upon the undying Atman. They realised that 'like corn, a mortal ripens and like corn is born again' (*Katha Upanishad*). The human entity is born again and again across the aeons, gathering a multitude of experiences and gradually moving towards the possibility of perfection. This immortal spark they called the 'Atman'.

Having perceived the existence of the undying Brahman without and the undying Atman within, the great seers were able to make the critical leap of realising through their spiritual insight that the Atman and Brahman were essentially one. This is the third tenet of Hinduism. In the *Chhandogya Upanishad*, there is the famous story of Shvetaketu, who is taught by his father in a series of statements which end with the famous words *Tat tuam asi*—that thou art—meaning that the Atman was essentially the Brahman. What the exact relationship between the two is has been the basis of various great schools of Vedanta, some holding with Shankaracharya that in fact the two are identical (the *Advaita* Vedanta), some with Ramanujacharya that they are both unitary and dual (the *Vishishtadvaita*), and some with Madhavacharya that they are similar but always separate (the *Dvaita*).

Having established the existence of the Brahman, the Atman, and their relationship, the fourth major tenet of Hinduism is that the supreme goal of life lies in spiritual realisation whereby the individual becomes aware of the deathless Atman within him. The realisation of the Atman at once brings an entirely new dimension into the picture, and the realised soul transcends the cycle of suffering, illness, old age, and death, which are inevitable concomitants of ordinary life—the wheel of change and decay of the manifested universe. He may still choose to stay within the limits of manifestations, and by his presence sweeten the bitter sea of suffering, but he is no longer bound to do so.

The fifth tenet which lies at the very heart of the Hindu way of life is that of karma, a concept that includes action, causality, and destiny. Action being inevitable, the human individual is bound by the results of his actions, pleasant fruits flowing from good deeds and unpleasant consequences from evil ones. Karma can thus be considered the moral equivalent of the law of conservation of energy or the equivalent of action and reaction in the field of natural sciences. While it is true that what we are today is the result of our past deeds, it also follows that we are the makers of our future by the way we act at present. Thus, far from implying fatalism as is often wrongly believed, karma gives tremendous responsibility to the individual and places in his own hands the key to his future destiny. Naturally, the unerring law of karma can work itself out only over a sufficiently long period of time; therefore, the Hindu belief in reincarnation, with the Atman being reborn in a long series until the attainment of liberation. Indeed, if man were to have only one life, there would seem to be no moral or spiritual justification at all for the tremendous disparities and evidently undeserved suffering, even of children, which is so evident all around us. As the Bhagavad Gita has it: 'As a man casts off his worn-out garments and takes others that are new, so the Atman casts off worn-out bodies and enters others that are new.'

The Key Concepts

In addition to the Vedas and the Upanishads, Hinduism has a vast corpus of auxiliary scriptures including the two great epics, the *Ramayana* and the *Mahabharata*. Between them they express the collective wisdom and history of the entire race, and have had a profound influence on all aspects of Hindu life and culture in India and throughout Southeast Asia for over three thousand years. Then there are eighteen Puranas, rich in myth and symbol, of which the best known is the *Srimad Bhagavatam*; the Brahma-Sutras, which contain Vedantic philosophy in the form of aphorisms; and the Tantras, dealing with the esoteric aspects of the spiritual quest. There are also the codes of conduct, including the elaborate *Manu-Smriti*, which seek to relate religion to the social and individual lives of Hindus.

Embedded within the huge compass of the *Mahabharata* is that crest-jewel of Hindu thought and one of the great religious classics of mankind, the Bhagavad Gita. Before going into the teaching of the Gita, however, it will be useful to mention five sets of concepts which are an integral part of the Hindu ethos, as some understanding of these is essential if one is to grasp the main thrust of the teaching of the Gita. Briefly, the concepts are as follows:

The Four Yugas or Cycles of Time

The Hindu concept of time is cyclical, not linear. The universe is *anadi-ananta*, without beginning and without end, going through recurrent phases of manifestation and dissolution.

It is quite extraordinary how the Hindu concept of time is becoming more comprehensible with recent developments in extragalactic cosmology. Each day of Brahma, the creator principle in the Hindu trinity, consists of four billion, three hundred and twenty million years, and the night of Brahma is of a similar duration. Thus, the entire universe is a process of the outbreathing and inbreathing of Brahma, corresponding to alternating periods of manifestation and dissolution. Each manifested cycle is divided into four yugas or aeons—Satya, Treta, Dvapara, and Kali. In the Satya-yuga, virtue is in the ascendant, but this diminishes progressively until in the Kali-yuga it virtually disappears. At the end of each Kali-yuga, there is tremendous destruction, *pralaya*, after which the golden age appears again. The four yugas taken together form a Maha-yuga or a great cycle. We are now believed to be living in the Kali-yuga of the present cycle.

The Four Ashramas or Stages of Life

In the Hindu view, human life is divided into four ashramas or stages—Brahmacharya, Grihastha, Vanaprastha, and Sannyasa. As the ideal lifespan of each Hindu is supposed to be a hundred years, each of these stages consists of a twenty-five-year period. The first twenty-five years are spent as a student in the Brahmacharya stage, when the young man is expected to spend his time and energy upon the attainment of education at the feet of a qualified teacher, and to observe sexual abstinence. Once this is completed, he moves on to the Grihastha ashrama, or householder stage, wherein he marries, raises a family, and participates in economically productive activity for the welfare of society. By fifty, he is ready to move on to the Vanaprastha stage of semi-retirement, in which he gradually detaches himself from worldly activities to concentrate upon the study of scriptures and meditational practices. Finally, at seventy-five, he is ready to withdraw entirely from social life and become a sannyasi or ascetic by renouncing the world, freeing himself from all social responsibilities, and concentrating exclusively upon the spiritual quest. Sannyasa ashrama, however, can be entered into even at a younger age by a person who renounces worldly life and joins one of the many monastic orders that exist in Hinduism.

The Four Purusharthas *or Goals of Life*

According to Hindu thought, these four goals are *dharma*, *artha*, *kama*, and *moksha*. *Dharma* is a word that has often been translated as 'religion', but, in fact, it is more comprehensive. It implies not only a religious and philosophical framework but a total worldview, including a scheme of right conduct under various circumstances. It comes from the Sanskrit root *dhri*, which means to uphold, and in the broadest sense is used for the universal laws of nature that uphold the cosmos. It also implies such concepts as justice, virtue, morality, righteousness, law, and duty. It is the first of the four goals, because it is the most comprehensive and is valid throughout the life of a human being.

Artha, or wealth, is the second goal. It is interesting that Hinduism not only tolerates the importance of wealth but accepts it positively as one of the four main goals of life, provided its acquisition and utilisation are in accord with the enjoyment. Here again, Hinduism gives an important place to sensual enjoyment, realising that, while renunciation may be suitable for the ascetic, it is certainly not suited to the common man. Therefore, the concept of *kama*, or desire/pleasure, is incorporated in the Hindu ethos, and indeed it has its own shastra in the form of the famous *Kama-Sutra* by Vatsyayana.

The final goal in Hindu thought is *moksha*, or release from suffering, old age, and ultimately from death itself. As mentioned earlier, *moksha* is not simply a question of survival after death, which in any case is taken for granted in Hinduism; it implies transcending both life and death by the attainment of that spiritual poise whereby man is liberated from the wheel of *samsara*.

The Four Varnas or Castes

According to the traditional Hindu view, human beings are divided into four categories on the basis of their intrinsic qualities. The highest caste consists of Brahmins, the thinkers, philosophers, priests, whose role it is to provide spiritual guidance and intellectual sustenance to society. Next come the Kshatriyas, or warriors, whose *dharma* revolves around ruling the nation and defending it against aggression. Third are the Vaishyas, or traders, who are involved in agricultural and commercial operations, while all that falls within the sphere of service is the responsibility of the fourth category of Shudras, or labourers.

It is interesting that the word varna also means colour, and, if one looks back over the history of early India, it is clear that the problem of colour—as between the Aryans, the great existing Dravidian civilisation, and the numerous aboriginal tribes—was a major factor in the development of this caste concept. There were certain categories beyond the pale of the caste system, which were known as the outcastes, and whose ill-treatment over the centuries is a standing disgrace to the otherwise remarkable achievements of the Hindu civilisation.

The Four Yogas or Paths to the Divine

The word yoga is derived from the root *yuj*, meaning to join or yoke, and it involves the joining of the Atman with the Brahman, of the individual soul with the universal divine being. In the Hindu view, there are several methods of this union, and each spiritual aspirant chooses the one that is best suited to his inner and outer conditions. While the path is essentially one, it varies to the extent that emphasis is placed upon different human faculties. Over the ages, four main yogas or paths have developed—jnana, bhakti, karma and raja.

Jnana, or gyana, is the path of intellectual discrimination, suitable for those whose intellects are highly developed and who are taught constantly to discriminate between the real and the unreal, the ephemeral and the eternal, until they reach spiritual realisation. Bhakti, or the path of devotion to a personal form of god, is based on the emotional urge, and involves harnessing of the sovereign power of love to spiritual quest. In this path, there is a deep emotional relationship between the human and the divine, beautifully expressed by Arjuna in the Gita as the combined relationship of a father to a son, a friend to a dear friend, and a lover to his beloved. Karma, or the way of action, is best suited for people who are particularly drawn to social service, alleviation of human suffering, and organisational activity, and whose constant compulsion for work is directed towards the divine. Finally, Raja-yoga involves various spiritual practices, including physical and psychic exercises set out in Patanjali's classic, the Yoga-Sutra. These paths are by no means mutually exclusive, and can, indeed, enjoy a benign symbiosis.

Another important aspect of Hindu thought is the concept of the avatara, or descent of god in human form. In keeping with its concept of cyclic time, Hinduism holds that there have been numerous such descents in the past and there will be more in the future. As Krishna himself says in the Gita:

> *Whensoever righteousness declines, O Bharata, and unrighteousness arises, then do I manifest myself upon earth. For the deliverance of the good, for the destruction of evil-doers and for the re-establishment of righteousness, I am born from age to age.*

With these concepts in mind, we can now turn to the Bhagavad Gita. The teaching of the Upanishads is in a peaceful setting, usually in the forest ashramas or retreats of the teacher. The setting of the Bhagavad Gita, however, is entirely different. Here the teacher and the disciple—Shri Krishna and Arjuna—are placed in the very centre of the battlefield. The conches have been sounded, the flight of missiles has begun and, poised between the two armies, Arjuna suddenly suffers a failure of nerves when he sees arrayed against him, his kinsmen and teachers. He is overcome by a great wave of revulsion, and at that critical juncture implores his friend and teacher to show him the correct path. The setting of the Gita is thus similar to the present human predicament. Man today finds himself in the midst of serious conflicts, both outer and inner; and it is on the battlefield of life that he needs correct guidance. This explains the special appeal of the Gita to modern man.

Another unique feature of the Gita is that it fuses the four paths into a single integral movement towards the divine. It deals with all the four yogas, but constantly seeks to integrate them around the overriding relationship between Arjuna and Shri Krishna, the human and the divine. While the Brahman of the Upanishads is impersonal and is, therefore, referred to as 'That', in the Gita, Shri Krishna himself appears as the Divine Being that transcends both the manifest and the unmanifest in his all-encompassing consciousness. The divine in the Gita is not a non-personalised concept, but involves the personality, raised as it were to the nth degree. Thus, at the end of the teaching, Shri Krishna instructs Arjuna in these words:

The Lord, O Arjuna, is seated in the heart of all beings,
causing by His divine power the entire cosmos
to revolve as if mounted on a machine.
Take refuge in Him with your entire being, O Bharata;
by His Grace you will gain supreme peace and the eternal abode.

Having thus spoken of the divine in the third person, Krishna completes the teaching with the following memorable verse:

> *Fix your mind on Me, be devoted to Me,*
> *Sacrifice to Me, bow to Me and to Me shall you come.*
> *This is My pledge to you, for you are dear to Me.*
> *Abandon all dharmas and take refuge in Me alone.*
> *Fear not, I will deliver you from all sin.*

The Bhagavad Gita is a remarkable fount of inspiration and power. Among its many memorable passages is the famous scene in the eleventh chapter where Krishna reveals to Arjuna his Divine Form which encompasses the entire cosmos and yet includes the great calm that lies behind all manifestation. It is this vision that is described as having the splendour of a thousand suns risen simultaneously in the sky. The Gita also contains the celebrated and oft-quoted statement with regard to action and its fruit: 'while man should work constantly for the welfare of the world, he should not be attached to the fruits of his action and should repose them in the divine.' The Gita thus teaches unceasing involvement in action while retaining an inner core of detachment, and dedicating the totality of human life to the divine will. Involvement without obsession is the key concept.

While there are many avataras in the Hindu scriptures, including manifestations of Shiva in the south Indian tradition, the best known list is a set of ten incarnations of Vishnu known as the *Dashavatara*. These have had a profound influence on popular Hinduism, and include two of the most popular and widely worshipped figures in the Hindu pantheon, Rama and Krishna. Interestingly, these ten incarnations represent the evolutionary ladder in a most remarkable manner: they start with Matsya, the fish; then Kurma, the amphibious tortoise; then Varaha, the boar; then Narasimha, the man-lion; then Vamana, the dwarf; then Parashurama, the wielder of the great axe; then Shri Rama, the noble hero of the *Ramayana*; then Shri Krishna, the divine flautist and charioteer of the *Mahabharata*; then the Buddha; and in the final incarnation of this cycle yet to manifest, the Kalki avatara, depicted as a magnificent youth riding a great white horse with a meteor-like sword raining death and destruction on all sides, perhaps symbolising some cataclysmic nuclear conflict.

The inclusion of the Buddha as the ninth incarnation needs special comment, because it reveals the great capacity in Hinduism to absorb even heretical movements. Evidently the fame and influence of the Buddha were so great that he could not be ignored, and yet his teachings were in some respects antithetical to classical Hinduism. He was, therefore, absorbed into the Hindu pantheon, so that he is revered today by Hindus with no difficulty at all. Indeed, although technically the number of Buddhists in India is very small, this is partly due to the fact that many of his teachings, such as his stern condemnation of animal sacrifice, have become part of the Hindu mainstream itself. To some extent, the same can be said about Christ, and most Hindus have no difficulty in accepting him as one of the incarnations of god. What Hinduism is not able to accept is the exclusive claim of any one teacher to the monopoly of divinity and wisdom for all time to come.

Classical Hinduism

With the Vedas, the Upanishads, and the auxiliary scriptures culminating in the Bhagavad Gita, the major contours of Hinduism became clearly defined. But in Hinduism there has been through the last two thousand years a continuous process of reinterpretation and restatement by a series of remarkable men and women. Some were kings and erudite scholars, others were common folk, often unlettered and unsophisticated. Some belonged to the 'higher' Brahmin, Kshatriya, and Vaishya castes, others to the 'lower', including the 'outcastes'. Some spoke chaste Sanskrit, that most magnificent of human languages; others sang in the local dialects. Some lived in great palaces and temples; others in simple cottages, or roamed the countryside with neither home nor shelter. Some were devoted to Shiva, the great Lord seated in majestic solitude on the mountain peak; some to Krishna, the eternal lover playing his divine flute in the forests of Vrindavana. Some worshipped the great Mother in one of her innumerable forms, beauty enthroned upon the seat of power; others offered their homage to one or the other numerous deities in the Hindu pantheon, rich with an inexhaustible store of symbol and image.

And yet, running through all these remarkable persons like a golden thread, is the overriding common factor—their realisation of the divine. Hinduism has always reserved its deepest veneration for those who have in some way realised the divine. Scholars are respected, rulers are feared, but real veneration is reserved only for the realised ones who constitute a race apart, the race that never dies. And it is a remarkable fact, largely responsible for the continued vitality of Hinduism through the ages, that it has in every century produced a number of such realised souls. Spread from Kashmir in the north to Kerala in the south, from Gujarat in the west to Assam in the east, these great souls have by the sheer force of their spiritual realisation kept the inner power of Hinduism intact and reillumined Hindu society in times of incredible adversity and ordeal. Had it not been for these great ones, truly the salt of the earth, Hinduism which had to undergo such savage persecution for centuries would have vanished from the face of this earth.

The Great Acharyas

In a survey of the more important developments in Hinduism over the last twenty centuries, the first outstanding figure that comes to mind is Tiruvalluvar (AD 300), the great Tamil saint, whose classic work, the *Tirukural*, is generally known as the Veda of the Tamils. Then came Adi Shankaracharya (AD 686), the extraordinary philosopher from Kerala, who wrote illuminating commentaries on the great Hindu texts, innumerable hymns to various deities in beautiful Sanskrit, and a number of treatises on the philosophy of non-dualism or Advaita Vedanta. He also founded four *pithas* or monastic centres in the four corners of India—at Shringeri in the south, Dwarika in the west, Badrinath in the north, and Puri in the east—which have played a profound role in sustaining classical Hinduism down the ages. Shankara stressed the supreme importance of liberation achieved through knowledge which, in turn, is born of asceticism and meditation. In his system, devotion and action could only play a preparatory and subsidiary role.

In sharp contradistinction to Shankara's monistic philosophy was the theistic approach of the great Tamil scholar Ramanuja (AD 1017) who advocated qualified monism and proclaimed that the way of devotion was the supreme path. The seeker must develop a devotion to god so intense that he realises that he is only a fragment of Him and wholly dependent on His grace. Thus, Ramanuja held that, however high the individual soul may rise, it will always remain in some degree separate from the divine, so that the intense interpersonal relationship can subsist for ever.

Another great south Indian Acharya was Madhava (AD 1199), whose system can be described as dualistic in that he held that god and individual souls are eternally distinct, and the salvation consists not in the merger of the two but in the soul dwelling eternally close to god and enjoying the contemplation of His glory. Madhava also held a doctrine, not generally found in Hinduism, that souls who consistently indulge in evil can ultimately get so weighed down that they can be permanently expelled from the universe to a state of eternal damnation.

These great teachers and their followers wrote original commentaries upon the *prasthanatrayi*, the three foundations of Hindu philosophy—the Upanishads, the Brahma-Sutras and the Bhagavad Gita. In addition, for intellectual and academic classification, Hindu philosophy has been divided into six systems of thought, each associated with a great teacher, which are generally reduced to three categories. The Vaisheshika of Kanada and the Nyaya of Gautama form one group; the Sankhya of Kapila and the Yoga of Patanjali the second; and the Purva-Mimamsa of Jaimini and the Vedanta (also called Uttara-Mimamsa) of Vyasa the third. These schools are regarded as *astika* or orthodox, because they accept the overriding authority of the Vedas, while the two other great schools of Indian philosophy, Jainism (whose twenty-fourth great teacher, Mahavira, lived in the 6th century BC) and Buddhism (founded by Gautama Buddha in the same century) are regarded as *anastika* or heterodox because they repudiate the authority of the Vedas.

Almost contemporaneous with these great sons of Indian spiritual movements there developed in Kashmir a unique and extremely rich tradition, known to the world as Kashmir Shaivism. Based on the Tantras—esoteric spiritual texts—rather than the Vedas, it produced a series of great teachers, the most outstanding of whom was Acharya Abhinavagupta (AD 950-975), who must rank as one of the greatest spiritual masters in the entire Hindu tradition.

The Forms of the Formless

It is necessary to point out, however, that while learned scholars proclaimed and disputed these various schools of philosophy, for the common man, the mainstay of Hinduism has always been devotion to a deity representing some aspect or incarnation of the divine. Hinduism has a wealth of imagery, symbolism, and iconography, and has produced a dazzling array of images and concepts which often baffles non-Hindus. This has led to the erroneous view, still extant in some quarters, that Hinduism is polytheistic. It certainly encourages the worship of many forms and symbols, but it must be understood that behind these myriad forms is the same all-pervasive divinity mirrored in a thousand different ways.

Very briefly, popular Hindu worship today revolves around three major deities—Shiva, Vishnu as himself and his major incarnations, and the goddess. Shiva Mahadeva is the great primeval lord, and there is reason to believe that he is of a pre-Aryan origin because on the still undeciphered seals of the Indus Valley Civilisation (5000-3000 BC); there is a figure seated cross-legged with several of the features associated with Shiva. Shiva is invariably worshipped along with a lingam, a powerful symbol representing the creative force behind all manifestation. He is generally portrayed as a resplendent ascetic sitting in meditation on a mountain peak, his body smeared with ashes, deadly snakes entwined around his neck, and the sacred Ganges flowing from his matted locks. He is also worshipped in his role as the cosmic dancer, Nataraja, whose dance symbolises the eternal wheel of the cosmos where millions of worlds are destroyed every moment and millions other spring into existence to the best of the eternal rhythm. Indeed, the magnificent image of the dancing Shiva represents one of the high watermarks of human art.

Despite his fearsome appearance, Shiva (the very word means 'auspicious') is easy to please, Ashutosha, and is generous with his boons even to the titans who often misuse them. He is neither born nor does he die, being the master of birth and death. In south India, there is a tradition in which Shiva is believed to have appeared in human form on several different occasions, either to help his devotees or to impart esoteric teachings. He is the maha-yogi, the great ascetic, and the patron-saint of those practising yoga.

Shiva is the third god of the Hindu trinity—Brahma the creator, Vishnu the preserver, and Shiva the destroyer—but again it must be remembered that these are not three different gods but three aspects of the same divine being. This is beautifully portrayed in the magnificent monolithic sculpture of Trimurti on the Elephant Island off the coast of Mumbai. One of the world's great artistic creations, this massive sculpture shows clearly the three aspects integrated in a single, divine entity. In fact, the great art of India provides as useful a way of approaching an understanding of the theistic concepts as the texts themselves. Apart from sculpture and painting, the great classical dance forms of India, particularly the Bharatanatyam, can bring to life concepts which may appear abstruse and unidimensional when approached purely through the written word.

Vishnu is depicted as lying on a great serpent that floats on the vast, endless ocean of milk, the *kshirasagara*. In this form he is worshipped in many temples, especially in the south, but elsewhere in India he is more widely worshipped in two of his most popular incarnations associated with the two great epics—Shri Rama and Shri Krishna. Indeed, these two names have carried the undying message of Hinduism to billions of men and women for thousands of years now, not only in India but wherever the Hindu cultural impact has been felt in the world. Shri Rama is depicted with a bow in hand, accompanied by his noble wife Sita, his faithful brother Lakshmana, and his devoted follower, the monkey god, Hanuman. Shri Krishna is depicted in numerous forms, commencing with his early childhood as a baby, Bala Krishna, and terminating as the charioteer of Arjuna, Parthasarathi. But his most popular and appealing form is as a beautiful cowherd youth, Gopala Krishna, dark and resplendent, standing with one foot crossed over the other and playing his magic flute. He is generally worshipped along with Radha, the shepherdess who has come to symbolise the essence of the Krishna cult of devotion. Vishnu is also worshipped in some of his lesser known incarnations such as Narasimha, the man-lion, who appeared to rid the world of the demon-king, Hiranyakashipu, and save his son, the great boy-devotee Prahlada.

The third major focus of devotion in India is the goddess in her numerous forms. She is worshipped as Parvati, the consort of Shiva; Lakshmi, the consort of Vishnu; Sita and Radha along with Shri Rama and Shri Krishna. But, and this is a point of considerable significance, she is not only worshipped as a consort, but in her own right as the essence of power and beauty; as Durga with eighteen arms riding a lion and scattering the demon hordes like chaff; as Kali, the fierce, naked goddess standing upon a corpse and drinking the blood of her freshly slain enemies; as Saraswati, the goddess of art, poetry, and music, the patron of all learning and wisdom. The worship of the great mother is, of course, known throughout the world in one form or another, but it is in Hinduism that she appears in all her splendour.

There is a Puranic myth about the birth of Durga which is full of symbolic significance. Once a great demon, the buffalo-headed Mahishasura, representing the evil forces of brute materialism, succeeded in defeating all the gods (devas: the shining ones) and established his supremacy over creation. The gods despaired, because despite all their efforts, they could not vanquish this terrible monster. At last, they gathered together on a mountain peak and decided to pool their divine powers. Each god contributed his own power symbolised by a weapon, led by the lord of the gods, Indra. At the end of the great ritual when all the divine powers had been pooled, there arose a dazzling light which spread its glory throughout the three worlds. In the midst of the light appeared Durga, the great goddess, with a weapon in each of her eighteen arms, and riding a ferocious tiger. She then gave battle to Mahishasura, and after a terrible conflict lasting nine days and nine nights, she finally slew him and rid the world of this great terror. These nine nights, the Navaratri, are still celebrated every year by Hindus as symbolising the victory of divine power over the forces of evil.

In addition to Shiva, Vishnu, and the goddess, there are numerous other deities who are the object of devotion and worship by Hindus down to the present day. These include the elephant-headed Ganesha, remover of obstacles, whose worship is essential before any auspicious undertaking can begin; Kartikeya or Subrahmanya, the younger son of Shiva and Parvati who is widely worshipped in south India as a young boy with a spear, riding a peacock; Hanuman, the devoted follower of Shri Rama who, despite his simian appearance, is wise and powerful; Dattatreya, the three-headed deity who is the patron-saint of yogis engaged in esoteric practices; and Ayappan, a south Indian deity, believed to be the result of a union between Shiva and Vishnu in his female form as Mohini. Surya, the sun-god, is known as the *pratyaksha*-deva, the visible god, and is generally worshipped through the famous gayatri mantra. Curiously, Brahma, the first god of the Hindu trinity, has only one temple in Pushkar dedicated to him in all of India, his worship having evidently fallen into disuse along with that of the other Vedic gods such as Indra and Varuna.

An important point to remember is that the worship of these various deities is by no means mutually exclusive. While each Hindu usually has a special family deity—the *ishta-devata*—he often worships three or four different deities during his daily prayers, and pays homage to any deity in a temple he may visit. Also, apart from anthropomorphic deities, some Hindus in addition use certain symbols for purposes of meditation. The most important of these is the Aum which is described in the scriptures as being the audio-visual symbol of Brahman itself, and is endowed with a wealth of symbolism. An entire Upanishad—*Mandukya*—has been devoted to the word Aum, or Om.

Meditation on the symbol and sound of Aum is an important aspect of yoga, a word that has gained much currency of late throughout the world but is generally imperfectly understood. As has been mentioned earlier, yoga implies the joining or yoking of human consciousness to the Divine Being, and in this sense it can be applied to the four major paths of spiritual attainment. In a more specialised sense, yoga involves physical and mental disciplines directed at control over mental and physical functions, specially breathing. The classic text of this yoga is the celebrated Yoga-Sutra of Patanjali, one of the world's great religious classics.

The sutras, or aphorisms of Patanjali, lay down an eight-fold path, ashtanga-yoga of physical, psychological, and moral discipline that, if properly adhered to under the guidance of a qualified teacher, results in the consciousness of the seeker being gradually elevated until the Atman shines forth in its pristine glory as pure consciousness. This path also involves arousal of the kundalini shakti or serpent power, believed to be located at the base of the human spine. As this power rises through a series of occult centres or chakras located in various parts of the body, the consciousness is correspondingly elevated, until finally it bursts into the highest chakra at the top of the brain—the *sahasrara* or thousand-petalled lotus—where the merger between the Atman and the Brahman takes place and the seeker is plunged into the highest bliss. This elevated state, known as samadhi, is the goal of all yogic practices.

Numerous other texts on various aspects of yoga are to be found in Hindu literature, all basing themselves upon the foundations laid by Patanjali. These include the Tantras or esoteric texts which deal with the various practices and techniques of kundalini arousal and acquisition of psychic powers. These miraculous powers, or siddhis, are accepted as an important aspect of yogic practices, but their misuse or even excessive demonstration is frowned upon as a hindrance to the achievement of the supreme goal. Through the ages, as today, there have been in India a fair number of persons who possess these powers, and miracle-mongering has always been an occupational hazard for yogis which is not always easy to avoid.

An important aspect of Hinduism, whether it is yoga or any other system of philosophy, discipline or teaching, is the critical importance that is assigned to the guru or teacher. The guru in the Hindu tradition is to be venerated even more than one's parents, because while our parents give us physical life, it is the guru who brings about our spiritual rebirth whereby alone can man fulfil his cosmic destiny. This notion, which appears to many to be somewhat exaggerated, will become clearer when it is understood that the human guru is but a symbol of the divine power that already resides within us. The word guru itself means dispeller of darkness, and by bringing the light of spiritual wisdom into the material darkness of normal human consciousness, the guru indeed performs a unique and priceless function. Needless to say, in Hinduism, as in so many other religions, there is the usual quota of charlatans and even criminals masquerading under the guise and habit of spiritual teachers. Generally, a person gets the sort of guru he deserves, and there is a well-established tradition that when the disciple is ready, the guru will appear. In the *Mundaka Upanishad* two essential qualifications of a true guru are laid down, both of which must be fulfilled if a person is really to occupy that elevated status. The guru must be *shrotriya*, learned in the scriptures, and *brahmanishtha*, established in the Brahman or divine consciousness. Hinduism believes that spiritual attainment is not possible without a guru, although sometimes in place of a human guru, a book or scripture may suffice. There have also been instances in which people have been initiated by some high being through a dream rather than in the flesh.

The Bhakti Movement

Despite great turmoil for many centuries in the north, due to foreign invasions and conquests, Hinduism continued to develop. Indeed, an important aspect of its development during Muslim rule was a two-fold movement: a turning inwards to preserve itself in the face of challenge, and sometimes persecution, from orthodox Islam, which forbade many of the practices central to Hinduism, especially image-worship; and a syncretic movement in which at the mystical level there could be a synthesis between the two faiths. Both these factors led to a tremendous devotional revival which has collectively come to be known as the Bhakti movement, one of the most interesting movements in the long and eventful history of Hinduism.

Throughout the Middle Ages there arose a series of extraordinary saint-singers who preached the gospel of divine love and ecstasy. While previous Hindu teachings had been almost exclusively in Sanskrit, this new movement broke away from the rigid and conservative Brahmin-dominated tradition, and used the regional languages and dialects to propagate their message. This also involved a revolt against the rigid caste restrictions and taboos that had become a negative feature in classical Hinduism. The saint-singers not only came from all castes and communities, including Muslims and some remarkable women, but their message was addressed to the common people irrespective of caste or creed.

In Islam also, as against the ulama or clergy, there has always been a mystical tradition of seekers intoxicated with the love of god. These were known as Sufis, and it was with the Sufi tradition that the Bhakti movement developed close affinity. The first major Sufi teacher to come to India was the great Khwaja Moinuddin Chishti (1143-1236). He arrived in Delhi towards the end of the 12th century, and finally settled in Ajmer where he had many disciples, both Hindu and Muslim. His great shrine there, the Dargah Shareef, is today one of the most important centres of Muslim pilgrimage, and draws numerous Hindu pilgrims also year after year.

In Hinduism the first great figure of medieval mysticism was Ramananda (1370-1440). Although a disciple of Ramanuja, Ramananda moved away from traditional orthodoxy, challenged caste divisions and began preaching in Hindi rather than in Sanskrit. One of his most illustrious disciples was Guru Ravidas who was a cobbler by profession. By sheer dint of spiritual merit, he rose to become one of the most respected religious teachers of his time, and still has millions of followers.

Ramananda's disciples came mainly from the lower castes, the most famous being Kabir, who is claimed both by the Hindus and the Muslims. The son of a Muslim weaver, Kabir (1440-1518) was drawn into the Bhakti movement at an early age. His songs struck at the roots of religious orthodoxy, ritualism, and intolerance. Kabir combined in himself the best of the Sufi and Bhakti traditions. One of his songs (translated by Rabindranath Tagore) contains the following stanzas:

O servant, where dost thou seek me?
O! I am beside thee.
I am neither in the temple nor in mosque;
I am neither in Kaaba nor in Kailasha,
Neither am I in rites and ceremonies,
Nor in yoga and renunciation.
If thou art a true seeker
Thou shalt at once see me,
Thou shalt meet me in a moment of time.
Kabir says, O Sadhu, God is the breath of all breath,
There is nothing but water at the holy bathing places,
I know that they are useless, for I have bathed in them,
The images are all lifeless, they cannot speak.
I know, for I have cried aloud to them.
The Purana and the Koran are mere words;
Lifting up the curtain, I have seen.
Kabir gives utterance to the words of experience;
He knows well that all other things are untrue.

Kabir had a tremendous influence upon the India of his day. Despite the fact that he was a lowly weaver, the sheer force of his spiritual realisation made him a focus of great veneration. There is an interesting, perhaps apocryphal, story about his death. Both the Hindus and the Muslims claimed his body, the former insisting that he be cremated and the latter that he be buried. When the shroud was removed, however, the body had disappeared and in its place was a heap of flowers. These were then divided between the contending parties; the Hindus carried off their share and cremated them with great devotion, while the Muslims buried their share with equal veneration. Thus, in death as in life Kabir taught the gospel of spiritual communion and brotherhood to India's two largest religious communities.

Kabir had many disciples, but two teachers who were greatly influenced by him deserve special mention. The first was Nanak (1469-1538) who went on to found the Sikh faith. He constantly emphasized that in the sight of god, 'there was no Hindu and no Muslim', and many of the hymns contained in the Granth Sahib, the sacred book of the Sikhs, echo this concept. Another of Kabir's followers was Dadu (1544-1603), who also founded a powerful movement based on his teachings known as Dadupanth. He wrote many beautiful hymns, and in one of them he says:

God is my ancestor, the creator is my kinsman,
The world-guru is my caste, I am a child of the Almighty.

The Bhakti movement produced a profusion of great literature. Two figures of particular importance in the vast Hindi-speaking Indo-Gangetic plain are Tulsidas (1527-1623) and Suradas

(1478-1581). Tulsidas produced the first great classic in Hindi, the *Ramacharitamanas* (Holy Lake of Rama's Deeds), which is the story of the *Ramayana* retold in Hindi verse with a wealth of poetry and deep devotion. There are many versions of the *Ramayana*, the most important being the original Sanskrit version of Valmiki and the Tamil version of Kamban. But the *Ramacharitamanas* has had a unique impact. For millions of Hindus in north India, it has provided for centuries the main cultural and religious foundations, and down to this day verses from it are sung in every village and town. It was this great religious classic that the indentured labourers, who went from India to Fiji, Surinam, Mauritius, and other plantations during colonial rule, took with them, and which remains their religious umbilical cord linking them to the land of their origin. Tulsidas looks upon Shri Rama as the supreme incarnation of the divine being, born for the salvation of mankind, and worthy of total devotion and dedication.

Suradas, considered by some critics to be an even greater poet, became blind in early childhood. None the less, he composed beautiful devotional poetry directed towards Shri Krishna. The descriptions of Krishna's childhood, his youthful pranks, his dalliance with the gopis (milkmaids) of Vrindavana, his magical feats, his resplendent personality epitomising the Divine Lover who summons human souls to the golden notes of his eternal flute, are part of the great heritage of Hinduism. Both Tulsidas and Suradas, along with a number of other devotional saints, including the Pathan Raskhan, another devotee of Shri Krishna, gave a tremendous boost to popular

Hinduism. At a time when Muslim rule was being established over most of India, and the older, classical orthodoxy was losing its hold upon the people's minds, the Bhakti movement once again demonstrated the resilience of Hinduism and its capacity to enable its followers to restate and reinterpret the eternal verities in the light of changed circumstances.

In Karnataka, the great saint Purandaradasa (1480-1564) sang of the glory of god and won a vast following. Eastern India, particularly Bengal, has always been an important centre of Hinduism. The great 11th century poet-devotee Jayadeva, who composed one of the post-classical Sanskrit masterpieces, the *Gita Govinda*, relating the story of Shri Krishna, had given a great fillip to Vaishnava worship in Bengal and Orissa. An extraordinary saint called Chaitanya (1485-1534), popularly known as Mahaprabhu (the Great Lord), and considered by his devotees to be an incarnation of Shri Krishna himself, founded the Vaishnava movement in Bengal. A special feature of his ministry was the kirtans, choral singing and chanting, by groups of devotees wandering from village to village and from town to town. Often the men involved in chanting would be carried away by a religious frenzy, and Shri Chaitanya himself would be thrown into a trance or fit of ecstasy as he contemplated the glory of Krishna. Although he did not write extensively, he exerted a profound influence on the subsequent development of Bengali and Oriya literature.

Further east, in the Brahmaputra Valley, another great teacher and reformer, Shankaradeva (1449-1568), writing in Assamese, greatly influenced the Hindus of that region. The same is true of Tukarama (1607-1649) in Maharashtra, which had earlier produced the young saint Jnaneshvar (1275-1296). whose Marathi work, the *Jnaneshvari*, is one of the great classics of Hinduism.

No survey of the Bhakti movement, howsoever brief, can omit the names of two remarkable women who have left the impress of their attainment upon future generations. Lalleshvari (1317-1372), also known as Lal Ded, was a Kashmiri saint who attained god-realisation at an early age, and whose life is full of legends and stories of miracles. Her utterances teach the direct path of realisation through intense love of the divine, renouncing attachment to worldly possessions and family ties, and rising above the dualities of caste and creed. She writes:

Shiva abides in all that is everywhere;
Then do not discriminate
Between a Hindu and a Muslim.
If thou art wise, know thyself;
That is the true knowledge of the Lord.
I renounced fraud, untruth, deceit;
I taught my mind to see the One
In all my fellowmen.
How could I then discriminate
Between man and man
And not accept the food
Offered to me by brother man?

The other great woman figure of the Bhakti movement was Mirabai (1450-1512), a Rajput princess who was married at an early age to the Rana of Udaipur. She was a childhood devotee of Shri Krishna, and had dedicated her life to him. After her marriage, she continued to devote her entire time to the worship of Krishna, incurring the displeasure of her husband who even tried to poison her. By Krishna's grace, however, the cup of poison turned into honey as she danced in ecstasy before the image of the god. Mira subsequently renounced her worldly life, and wandered through India singing her beautiful compositions, which are among the most moving devotional songs of Hinduism. One of her best loved hymns goes thus:

Tying anklets upon her feet,
Mira dances in ecstasy.
People say Mira has gone mad,
Her mother-in-law says she has disgraced the clan,
The Rana sent her a cup of poison
Which Mira, laughingly, drank.
I have myself become the eternal maid-servant of
My Narayana.
Mira's God is Giridhar, lifter of the mountain.
O Indestructible One, meet me swiftly in your
Eternal embrace.

Thus, we see that in its most difficult period Hinduism produced a glittering galaxy of saint-singers drawn from all corners of the country, who inspired millions by their devotion and poetry, presented in an idiom readily understood by the masses. They were re-stating the great Vedantic truths—the unity of Atman and Brahman, of the human and the divine—

in a new phraseology which took the message down to the most humble villages where the majority of Hindus have always lived. Their songs remain to this day a major source of inspiration for Hindus, and while the sonorous Sanskrit chanting of the magnificent Vedic hymns can still be heard on special occasions, especially in south India, it is the songs of the medieval saints which echo and re-echo in fields and forests, in villages and towns. Truly it has been said that music has the unique capacity to carry the human consciousness out of its narrow confines towards the brimming ocean of the Divine.

The Modern Renaissance

The entire history of Hinduism, looked at from a certain angle, can be seen as a constant process of challenge and response. To each major crisis, Hinduism reacted, first by briefly withdrawing into a shell, and then, with its unparalleled capacity for assimilation and regeneration, by a new resurgence. This happened with the Jain and Buddhist movements, with the early Christian missionaries and, to a lesser extent, with the Muslim advent. But with the arrival of the British, first as traders and finally as imperial rulers, Hinduism was confronted with the most critical of all the challenges it had faced in its long and eventful history.

By the time the British arrived in India, Hinduism had reached perhaps its lowest ebb. All sorts of superstitions and undesirable practices flourished in the name of religion. Caste taboos had become so rigid that Hindu society, which a thousand years earlier had sent its great missionaries to the four corners of Asia, had begun to insist on anyone returning from abroad having to undergo purification rites. Women, who once enjoyed an honoured position and are found in the Upanishads conversing freely with men upon the highest philosophical topics, had become virtual slaves in the joint family. Widows were treated with great cruelty, female infanticide was rife in some castes, and compulsory immolation of widows was often enforced. Theologically also, the great Vedantic truths that lay behind Hindu thought had been obscured by the jungle growth of superstition and corruption. The inspiration of the medieval saint-singers, while still prevalent, had begun to fade in the face of the political turmoil and widespread anarchy that followed the collapse of Mughal power. Indeed, it was one of the darkest periods in Indian history, and it seemed that Hinduism had at last exhausted its spiritual reserves, and would gradually fade away in the face of the new onslaught.

However, once again the miracle of regeneration was witnessed, and Hindu society produced a series of remarkable men who, by the sheer power of their spiritual illumination, rekindled the dying spark. In 1857, after what is commonly known as the Great Indian Mutiny, but which many now prefer to call India's First War of Independence, India lay crushed at the feet of her foreign, imperial conquerors, broken not only in body but also in spirit. People began to lose faith in their cultural and religious heritage, and a miasma of spiritual darkness pervaded the land. And yet, within a short span of ninety years, India not only rose phoenix-like from the ashes but swept to a triumphant freedom which marked the beginning of a global process of decolonisation. This achievement can, to a large extent, be traced to a resurgence of Hinduism. This is not to deprecate in any way the role of the other communities in India's national revival, but to highlight the fact that the majority of Indians have always been Hindus, and it is Hinduism, therefore, that predominantly set the tone of a national culture in India and provided the ethos, the cultural milieu, the great backdrop, as it were, against which the drama of her history was enacted.

It was in the great movement for social reform in Hinduism that the first creative reaction to British rule manifested itself, and it was Bengal, the first province in India to feel the brunt of British conquest, that spearheaded this cultural revival. It was here that the first of a long line of great leaders of thought and action arose, a man who has often been described as the 'pathfinder' of modern India. Raja Ram Mohun Roy (1772-1833) was a man of unusual intellectual ability, a profound scholar of Sanskrit and Persian, as well as a deep admirer of British culture. He took a leading part in starting English-medium schools in Bengal, and in 1828 founded the Brahmo Sabha, later to develop under his successor Devendranath Tagore into the Brahmo Samaj. This was the first deliberate attempt in modern India to reform Hinduism, and to cleanse it of the undesirable encrustation that had developed around it over the centuries.

The Brahmo Samaj, as well as its offshoots, the Adi Brahmo Samaj, led by Devendranath Tagore, the Brahmo Samaj of India founded by Keshub Chunder Sen in 1868, and the Sadharan Brahmo Samaj founded by some of his followers in 1878, all based themselves upon the pristine authority of the Vedas, and strongly attacked idol worship and undesirable social customs such as compulsory sati, immolation of widows upon their husband's funeral pyres. The leaders of the movement, especially Sen, were considerably influenced by the style of Christian missionaries who had become active under British rule, and many of their prayer meetings were modelled upon Christian church services.

Under the influence of the Brahmo Samaj, several such movements started in other parts of India, notably the Prarthana Samaj founded in Bombay in 1867 by the great scholars, M.G. Ranade and R. D. Bhandarkar. These societies, while influencing mainly the English-educated fringe of society, did play an important part in bringing a new intellectual awareness into Hindu society, and encouraged educated Hindus to re-examine their religious heritage in the light of changing conditions. The same is true of the Theosophical Society which was founded by Madame Blavatsky and Colonel Olcott in New York in 1875 and gained considerable popularity in India, largely through the work of Mrs. Annie Besant. Simultaneously, the rediscovery of the ancient Indian texts by European scholars such as Max Müller, Ferguson, and Cunningham, and the work of Western archaeologists and linguists which brought to light the remarkable achievements of the Hindu past that had virtually been lost during centuries of Muslim rule, helped to give the 19th century Hindu a new awareness of his rich cultural heritage and a renewed pride in his ancient religion.

All this, however, remained largely confined to the small, educated classes, awaiting a movement that would touch the heart of traditional Hinduism. This was not long in coming. A major figure in the Hindu revival was Swami Dayanand Saraswati (1824-83) who founded the Arya Samaj in 1875. Unlike the Brahmo and its offshoots, which were considerably influenced by Christianity, the Arya Samaj was militantly Hindu. Swami Dayanand passionately advocated a return to the pristine purity of Vedic Hinduism, and denounced with intolerant indignation the post-Vedic Hindu scriptures such as the Puranas. He also condemned idol worship and caste distinctions, advocated full equality for women, initiated a widespread educational campaign with special emphasis on female education, and launched a crusade against untouchability. Rightly described as a human dynamo, Swami Dayanand shook the structure of established Hinduism to its foundations and infused it with new blood and fresh vigour.

Numerous other reformist and educational movements in Hinduism developed in the second half of the 19th century. For purposes of this overview, however, we shall confine ourselves to a mention of five outstanding figures who have left their indelible impress upon modern Hinduism, and whose tremendous personalities have gone a long way in shaping the contours of the Hindu mind in our own century. These are Sri Ramakrishna, Swami Vivekananda, Mahatma Gandhi,, Sri Aurobindo, and Sri Ramana Maharshi . Each of these men, drawn from the very heart of the Hindu tradition, reinterpreted its eternal truths in the light of his own extraordinary attainment. Between them they achieved nothing less than a comprehensive revival of the best in the Hindu tradition, and collectively represent a major force in the contemporary religious thought of the world.

Sri Ramakrishna (1836-86)

Born in a poor Brahmin family in Hooghly district, West Bengal, Gadadhar Chattopadhyay, or Chatterjee, began showing unusual signs of religious ecstasy at a very early age. When he was nineteen, he came to Calcutta to live with his elder brother who had been appointed priest of a newly built temple at Dakshineshwar on the banks of the river Ganges. The main shrine is dedicated to the great goddess Kali, from which Kolkata derives its name, and it was as a devotee of the goddess that Sri Ramakrishna, as he came to be called, began his astounding career of spiritual discipline and attainments. Visions, trances, and ecstasies crowded in upon him, and most of his time was spent in intense spiritual rhapsodies. His agonised craving to see the Divine face to face was fulfilled, and he then proceeded under various spiritual guides to experience the whole gamut of mystical relationships described in the Hindu scriptures, ranging from intense emotional raptures to the supreme beatitude of the *nirvikalpa* samadhi—contact with the all-pervasive, formless Brahman which is the highest goal of Vedanta. Not content with this, he proceeded to adopt the spiritual practices of Christianity and Islam, and in both cases he has recorded that they culminated in sublime spiritual experiences connected with the founders of these two great faiths.

The cumulative effect of these extraordinary phenomena was immense. By the sheer force of his spiritual attainment, Sri Ramakrishna became a beacon-light in the encircling gloom of his time. Gradually, the fame of this unlettered young priest began to spread far and wide throughout Bengal. The villager and the city dweller, the scholar and the poet, the educated and the illiterate—people from all walks of life began finding their way to Dakshineshwar. Among them were some of the great luminaries from different walks of life in contemporary Bengal, men like Girish Ghose, Dr M.L. Sircar, Keshub Chunder Sen, Bijoy Krishna Goswami, Pandit Sasadhar Tarkachuramani, etc. On his own part, Sri Ramakrishna paid visits to illustrious persons like Devendranath Tagore, Iswar Chandra Vidyasagar, and Bankim Chandra Chatterjee.

To all who came, Sri Ramakrishna gave the same message. He exhorted them not to waste their time squabbling over this or that creed or religion, but to seek god with a pure and dedicated heart. He reaffirmed on the basis of his own spiritual experiences that all creeds and religions led ultimately to the same goal, and he expressed his teachings in a series of homilies and telling parables that made them intelligible to even the most unsophisticated villager. His sayings and the story of his life remain to this day a major source of religious inspiration.

Sri Ramakrishna showed that, far from being a dying religion as some of the newly educated intelligentsia had begun to believe, Hinduism was an inexhaustible fount of spiritual inspiration. Though he lived quietly in Dakshineshwar and seldom ventured outside the temple compound, his very presence generated a powerful current of fresh light into Hindu society. And the Bengalis, with their unusual emotional and intellectual capacities, responded eloquently to this saint. Sri Ramakrishna was, indeed, an apostle of divine realisation, one of those rare souls whose coming heralded a spiritual revolution.

Swami Vivekananda (1863-1902)

Apart from his influence upon those who occasionally visited Dakshineshwar, Sri Ramakrishna attracted a group of brilliant young disciples, several of them products of the new English schools and colleges that had been recently established in Bengal. Many of these young men had lost faith in their traditional religion and were wallowing in a sea of cynicism and spiritual despair. They found in Sri Ramakrishna a source of tremendous inspiration, a man who could banish their spiritual gloom and transform their very personalities. Outstanding among these disciples was young Narendranath Datta, later to be famous the world over as Swami Vivekananda.

One has to go all the way back to Socrates and Plato to find a parallel for the Ramakrishna-Vivekananda relationship. Though apparently poles apart from the master, it was the student who spread his teachings far and wide until they encompassed almost the entire world. Vivekananda was a man of remarkable qualities, gifted both with a powerful physique and outstanding intellect. Just before his death, Sri Ramakrishna designated Vivekananda his spiritual heir, and after his master's passing he took upon himself the task of knitting the disciples into a dedicated band. After wandering the entire length of India as a penniless ascetic seeking a way to propagate the ideals of his beloved master, Vivekananda heard of the Parliament of Religions that was to be held in Chicago in 1893 in connection with the World Fair. With considerable difficulty he succeeded in getting a passage to America, and after facing further hardships finally reached Chicago and enrolled himself as a delegate to the conference. His advent at the gathering had all the elements of high drama. An obscure and unknown Hindu monk, he succeeded by the very force of his personality in dominating the whole concourse which today is remembered mainly because of him. A powerful speaker with a sonorous voice and a fine command of English, Vivekananda's famous address on the first day of the Parliament created a sensation, and his subsequent speeches established him as an outstanding preacher.

In his short life of thirty-nine years, Swami Vivekananda undertook what was in effect a restatement of Hinduism in the light of the new situation that had developed during the 19th century. He travelled extensively in India and abroad, lecturing on the basic Vedantic principles that underlay Hinduism. He thundered against the 'Kitchen religion', the ridiculous taboos and restrictive customs that had overlaid the tremendous Vedantic truths. He reaffirmed not only the divinity of god but also the inherent divinity of man. A special feature of his teachings was his keen social conscience and his intense emphasis on service to the poor and the down trodden, the sick and the hungry. He often quoted the Rig

Vedic dictum of the human life having a two-fold aim—*atmano mokshartham jagat—hitaya cha*—for the welfare of the world and the salvation of one's soul. One of his celebrated remarks is that it was an insult to preach religion to a man with a hungry stomach, and that the only way god could appear before the masses of India was in the form of bread. He stressed the primacy of spiritual life, preached a doctrine of inner strength and spiritual power which alone could free India from her material, intellectual, and spiritual bondage, and stressed the essential unity of all religions.

Two features of Vivekananda's ministry merit special mention, as they had an abiding influence upon the revival of contemporary Hinduism. In 1897 he founded the Ramakrishna Math and Mission with headquarters at Belur near Kolkata. Although Hinduism had a long and distinguished monastic tradition going back to Adi Shankaracharya, the Ramakrishna Mission was a new order, and its approach to the problems of contemporary India was based on a modern reinterpretation of the ancient doctrines. It had a special bias towards educational and medical work, and has over the decades distinguished itself in providing relief to the victims of natural calamities such as floods and famine. In this respect, Vivekananda clearly modelled his organisation on the pattern of the Christian missionaries who had been active in India ever since the British advent. The Ramakrishna Mission today, with numerous branches in India and abroad, continues to play a significant role in spreading the gospel of Sri Ramakrishna and his great disciple.

The other feature of Swami Vivekananda's life was the contribution he made to the spread of Hindu thought abroad, especially in America. Prior to his advent, it was only a handful of Western Indologists and scholars who had any real insight into the Hindu ethos, while among the general public, there flourished all sorts of grotesque impressions regarding this great religion. Vivekananda pioneered a new awareness of Hinduism in the West. His eloquent and able presentation of the essential truths that underlie Hinduism, and his broad approach of the essential unity of religions, combined to make him a unique spokesman of the eternal East to the bustling technological culture of Western society.

Vivekananda had a deep conviction that India's goal was not only to achieve her own regeneration but also to give a new spiritual impetus and light to the world. Hinduism is not a proselytising religion; therefore, Vivekananda was not seeking converts. Rather, he sought to state the basic principles of Vedanta and allow their inner power to work upon the minds and hearts of his listeners. Indeed, he was the torchbearer of a whole new religious movement, and the forerunner of numerous other Hindu teachers and yogis who continue to this day to work in the West. Thus, both in India and abroad, Vivekananda, stands as a towering figure in modern Hinduism. His advocacy of 'neo-Vedanta', as it is sometimes called, gave a new direction to traditional Hinduism, and continues to have a profound influence upon contemporary religion.

Mahatma Gandhi (1869-1948)

Mahatma Gandhi is known throughout the world for his unique leadership of the Indian freedom movement, for the concepts of *satya* and *ahimsa* (truth and non-violence) which were the cornerstones of his political philosophy, and for the manner in which he was able to shake the foundations of the great British Empire. Indeed, the Indian freedom movement marked the end of the colonial era that had dominated the world scene for the preceding three centuries, and India's independence in 1947 heralded the emergence into freedom of dozens of other nations that had for long been the victims of colonial subjugation. Mahatma Gandhi is today revered in India as the Father of the Nation, and remains a source of not only inspiration in India but wherever man is still struggling for freedom.

It is useful to remember, however, that Gandhi's approach to politics was broadly based on Hindu principles. He was himself a devout Hindu, and will go down in history as one of the greatest social reformers that Hinduism produced. In a way he combined the two streams of thought—radical and moderate—in the freedom movement. While accepting the radicals' goal of Purna Swaraj or complete independence, he also breathed new life into the reform movements that the moderate leaders had espoused. Gandhi's main contribution to Hinduism was the manner in which he took up the problem of untouchables, whose ill-treatment had been one of the most disgraceful features of Hindu society. By renaming them as Harijans, or children of god, he made a symbolic gesture of atonement, and thereafter, he pursued a policy of living in Harijan colonies wherever he went, personally cleaning latrines and giving depressed classes a sense of self-esteem and involvement in the mainstream of Hindu society. The special reservations in legislatures, services, and educational institutions are a direct result of Gandhi's influence and the remarkable contribution of Dr B.R. Ambedkar, the Harijan, or Dalit, leader.

Another major contribution made by Gandhi was the involvement of women in large numbers in the freedom movement, and the stress he laid upon their social emancipation. His 'Constructive Programme', which included the propagation of handicrafts and cottage industries, also had an egalitarian effect upon Hindu society. All his prayer meetings began with Ram Dhun, chanting of the Lord's Name, and for his concept of the perfect government he went back to the Rama Rajya, the ideal rule in the ancient days of Sri Rama. He wrote a commentary on the Bhagavad Gita which he looked upon as a perennial source of inspiration. He encouraged the worship of the cow, not so much on religious grounds but as a symbol of the beneficent symbiosis between human and animal existence.

Gandhi's concept of 'truth' is deeply based on the Hindu tradition. The famous words of the *Mundaka Upanishad*—*satyam eva jayate* (truth alone triumphs)—constituted his motto. This was adopted as India's national motto after independence. His insistence on *ahimsa* also had its roots in one aspect of Hinduism, although this was stressed more in the Buddhist and Jain traditions. His autobiography, *My*

Experiments with Truth, is a remarkable document, and shows Gandhi's deep commitment to the fundamental ideals of Hinduism. While he never claimed to be a religious leader and always displayed the utmost humility in such matters, he was categorical in his assertion that for him religion had primacy over all other aspects, and that it was absurd to hold that politics had nothing to do with religion. He stressed the Hindu concept of the essential unity and harmony of all religions, and his prayer meetings would include readings from other religious scriptures in addition to those from Hinduism. He was greatly influenced by the saint-singers of medieval India, specially Kabir and Mirabai, and shared their direct and simple approach to religion of the masses.

During his three decades of political pre-eminence in India, Gandhi's contribution to the regeneration of Hinduism and the reform of Hindu society was monumental. He must, therefore, be ranked not only as a unique political leader but also as one of the main formative influences in modern Hinduism, a man who left the indelible impress of his personality not only upon his country but upon his religion as well.

Sri Aurobindo (1872-1950)

Born on 15 August 1872 in Calcutta, Aurobindo Ghosh was sent to school in England at the age of seven. There, first at the Manchester Grammar School, then at St. Paul's in London and finally at King's College, Cambridge, he underwent a full educational career covering fourteen years during which he passed the classics tripos in the first division and won college prizes for English and literary ability. He returned to India in 1893 at the age of twenty-one, and entered Baroda State Service as Professor of English, then became Vice-Principal, and later Principal of Baroda College.

Aurobindo was gifted with a brilliant mind and a deep psychic power. While in England he read the writings on the Irish Sinn Fein movement and the Italian Risorgimento. This filled him with a fervent sense of patriotism, and back home he began taking a keen interest in the freedom movement, still in its infancy.

In 1885 an Englishman, Alan Octavian Hume, founded the Indian National Congress, and soon there developed two clear trends of thinking in this great organisation, the 'moderates' who aimed at gradual transfer of power, and the 'extremists' whose ideal was full freedom at once. Aurobindo soon became a leader of the extremists along with Lokmanya B.G. Tilak, and in 1905, when the British pushed through the highly controversial partition of Bengal, he quit his Baroda job and plunged into the national movement. For five years, from 1905 to 1910, Aurobindo shone like a meteor on the political firmament. His brilliant editorials in the *Bande Mataram* and *Karmayogin*, patriotic journals he edited, are among the most outstanding of political writings in English. His political philosophy was deeply rooted in the Hindu tradition of mother-worship, particularly pronounced in Bengal. Drawing his inspiration from the famous Bengali novel *Ananda Math* by Bankim Chandra Chatterjee, written half a century earlier, and in particular from the poem 'Bande Mataram' (Hail to Thee, Mother) contained therein, Aurobindo developed a comprehensive political philosophy. The key concept was the divinity of the motherland, which he idealised as the goddess Bhavani Bharati, and flowing from that the concept of nationalism not simply as a political credo but as a spiritual imperative. The spiritual nationalism, expounded by him, had an electrifying effect upon the youth of Bengal and other parts of India at that crucial juncture; and, though the movement did not meet with immediate success, it brought about for the first time a mass involvement, and left an indelible impact upon the Indian freedom movement.

While at Baroda, Aurobindo had begun following some yogic practices, and during the Bengal agitation he was arrested in the celebrated Alipur Bomb Conspiracy Case and kept in jail for over a year. It was during this enforced solitude that the spiritual trend in his psyche gained predominance; and, though after his acquittal he continued for some time with political activities, he realised that his real life-work lay elsewhere. In 1910, on a sudden inner impulse, he left Bengal for the French colony of Chandernagore, and from there moved on to the other French colony of Pondicherry where he lived for forty years until his death in 1950. In the course of his four decades at Pondicherry, Sri Aurobindo developed one of the most comprehensive and original systems of thought in modern times. He based himself upon the Hindu tradition, but gave creative interpretations to the ancient texts including the Vedas and the Upanishads. His masterly work, *Essays on the Gita*, is perhaps the most outstanding of the many commentaries that have been written upon this sacred text since Shankaracharya, while his chief literary work, *The Life Divine*, the massive epic poem, 'Savitri,' and numerous other works stand as a testimony to his gigantic intellect and deep intuition.

If his political philosophy can be called spiritual nationalism, Aurobindo's general philosophy can well be called spiritual evolution. He rejects the traditional Hindu concept of individual salvation, and stresses those aspects of the Hindu tradition that speak of raising the collective consciousness of the race. The key concept in his thought is that of spiritual evolution. According to Sri Aurobindo, man is the result of aeons of evolution from unicellular organisms up through mineral, vegetable, and animal forms. However, he is by no means the end-product of evolution. Aurobindo postulates a further evolutionary thrust from man with his mental faculties to superman with supramental faculties. Indeed, he holds that it is only with the next quantum leap in the evolutionary adventure that mankind will break out of its present impasse and fulfil its spiritual destiny.

Aurobindo wrote at great length with regard to this leap, and presented for its fulfilment his own path which he called 'Integral Yoga' because it seeks to draw together the strands of the four traditional yogas into a single, multi-faceted spiritual endeavour. Aurobindo's goal was not individual salvation, not even racial salvation, it was nothing less than a fundamental change in the texture of terrestrial consciousness itself, the creation of 'a new heaven and a new earth'. Often described as the pioneer of the supramental, Aurobindo's 'Integral Yoga', worked out with the active collaboration of his companion, Madame Alfassa, known as the Mother, has three broad movements: first, a complete and integral surrender to the divine; second, a raising of the human consciousness to the supramental level; and, third, a return to earth after absorbing the power and light of the supramental so that its influence can be directly brought to bear upon terrestrial life. This stress on evolution, though based essentially upon Hindu texts, marks a new development in contemporary Hinduism which has still not fully unfolded itself.

Sri Ramana Maharshi (1879-1950)

If Sri Ramakrishna was a bhakta par excellence and Swami Vivekananda a karma-yogi, Sri Ramana was in the great Hindu tradition the gyana-yogi. Belonging to a middle-class Brahmin family of Tamil Nadu, Ramana, at the age of seventeen, had a series of powerful spiritual experiences that culminated in his taking up permanent residence at the holy Arunachala Hill with the town of Tiruvannamalai at its foot. Here he gradually started attracting a group of devotees, and lived for the rest of his life as a revered saint, or maharishi, recognised by all as a powerful figure on the spiritual firmament.

Sri Ramana's teachings expound the Vedantic path of self-knowledge, and his original works as well as commentaries upon the Hindu classics all flow from the process of self-enquiry. The question 'Who am I?' is to be found in most religious traditions, because the quest for self-knowledge is at the heart of every spiritual endeavour. But Sri Ramana made this the cornerstone of his whole philosophy. To every question he would respond by asking a counter-question. 'Who is it that asks?' Thus, when the body, the senses, the mind are all negated, the real 'I' begins to shine forth in all its glory.

This process of spiritual introspection was presented by Sri Ramana with great clarity, and he also taught a process of pranayama or breath control that would assist the seeker to still the modifications of the mind and focus the psychic energy upon asking that single question, 'Who am I?' He likened this 'to the flaming brand that is used to light a great fire; it not only sets the entire material ablaze but also consumes itself in the process. Thus, Sri Ramana taught that the question 'Who am I?' if properly and persistently asked, has the capacity to destroy all delusion and ultimately itself disappear with the dawn of spiritual realisation.

Unlike Vivekananda, Sri Ramana never concerned himself with social service or reform movements. He seldom ventured outside his abode at Arunachalam, and yet such was his spiritual presence that he commanded veneration from all sides. The thousands who trekked to see him were often content to do just that, because in the Hindu tradition even the sight of a holy person—darshana—has its own spiritual merit. Sri Ramana had an extraordinary presence. Quite unconcerned with outer events, he was as one permanently centred in the Brahman, and his words came not from intellectual brilliance but from a perfect inner assurance. Like Sri Ramakrishna before him, he was living proof of the spiritual power of Hinduism. It said that the night he passed away after undergoing a long and painful ailment with no sign of suffering or complaint, a bright comet moved across the sky and shone for a while in splendour above Arunachalam before disappearing behind the holy mountain.

In addition to these five outstanding personalities of modern Hinduism, numerous other major figures on the contemporary Hindu scene have made their contribution to the regeneration and re-interpretation of Hinduism. Most of them have founded their own societies and religious organisations. These include such persons as Yogananda Paramahansa who preached in America and founded the Yogoda Society; Swami Nikhilananda and Swami Prabhavananda of the Ramakrishna Mission in the US; Swami Sivananda of Rishikesh, who founded the Divine Life Society; Swami Bhaktivedanta Prabhupada, whose Krishna Consciousness movement has made such a mark in the West; and Sri Krishna Prem, an Englishman who has written glowing commentaries on the Bhagavad Gita and the *Katha Upanishad* and who, along with his guru Yashoda Mai, founded a Krishna temple near Almora in the Himalayas.

This list is by no means exhaustive, but is enough to show that Hinduism has always evolved through phases of creative resurgence. The great reformers knew that what is required in any faith and tradition is a reinterpretation of ancient truths in the light of contemporary compulsions. This, Hinduism has done time and again in its long and eventful history.

The Future

Mankind faces a complex dilemma at this stage of its evolution. Science and technology, if wisely used, have given man for the first time the capacity to abolish deprivation and poverty, illiteracy, disease, and inequality from the face of the earth. On the other hand, the same science has also given him the power to destroy not only the human race but perhaps all life. There is a great churning of the collective consciousness of humanity, and a tremendous urge for new certitudes to take the place of the old bulwarks that are collapsing. In such a situation, all religions face a fundamental challenge. Hinduism, with its tremendous capacity for regeneration and reinterpretation, should not have anything to fear. Indeed, India, with its rich and varied religious heritage as well as the most distinguished pool of scientific talent in the developing world, should be able to give the right lead to humanity at this crucial juncture.

The contribution of Hinduism, in the past, to world civilisation has been many-faceted. It covers, to mention just a few fields, mathematics (the discovery of zero or shoonya, which was the prerequisite for the technological marvels of the 20th and 21st centuries); medicine (through Ayurveda, one of the most ancient and integrated systems of medicine known to man); architecture (which produced such wonders as the rock-cut caves of Ellora and the great temple cities of south India); dance (with the Bharatanatyam and other classical dance forms based upon Bharata's great treatise, the *Natya Shastra*); music (both in the Carnatic and Hindustani traditions, which have had such an impact in recent years upon the West); psychology (through yoga, which represents the most profound inquiry into the mysteries of the human mind and psyche yet developed by man); linguistics and literature (through the vehicle of Sanskrit, unparalleled in its power and majesty, and other great languages, including Tamil); and of course, philosophy (from the luminous words of the Upanishads to Swami Vivekananda and Sri Aurobindo). In these and other fields too numerous to catalogue, the Hindu way has contributed to the corpus of human knowledge and attainment in a manner of which few religions can boast. Hinduism retains an inner dynamism and presents certain key concepts that are particularly relevant in this nuclear, and now Artificial Intelligence, age, not only for Hindus but also for the entire human race. The five seminal ideas that follow have been chosen for the breadth of their outlook that transcends religious and denominational barriers, and gives them universal relevance.

The Unity of Mankind

Every country has developed a love for its own nationhood, but there are few that have had the capacity to rise above the imposing mansion of nationalism and conceptualise the unity of the entire human race. It has been the Hindu genius that, although it has accepted and reiterated nationalism in the modern sense, particularly after the great renaissance in the 19th century, its best minds have always held up the concept of mankind as a single family, *vasudhaiva kutumbakam*, as the Rig Veda has it. The relevance of this to the present human predicament is obvious. Science and technology have now converted what was once only a vision in the minds of seers into a concrete reality. Time and space are shrinking before our eyes, and the first extraordinary photograph of earth taken from the moon showed our planet, as it really is, a tiny spaceship spinning in the endless vastness of space, so beautiful and yet so fragile. The essential unity of the race that inhabits this planet, based upon the fact of 'humanness' itself is thus a concept that is growing increasingly relevant as mankind struggles desperately to survive its own technological ingenuity.

The Harmony of Religions

The second great concept that Hinduism has developed through the ages is that of the harmony of religions. The yearning of the human for the divine, which is at the heart of the religious quest, has in practice often been translated into hideous strife between the followers of different religions, each convinced of its own righteousness and of cruel persecution within various religions themselves. The Hindu ethos, however, has always accepted different paths to the divine—*ekam sat viprah bahuda vadanti* (Truth is one, the wise call it by many names) as the Rig Veda has it. Apart from Hinduism, which has always been the predominant religion of India, there are millions of Muslims, Buddhists, Jains, Sikhs, Parsis, Christians (of several denominations), and Jews who have lived peacefully in this country for centuries. There are also famous shrines and pilgrimage-centres sacred to all these religions.

The unique synthesis achieved in Kashmir between the

Shaiva tradition and the Sufi influx, resulting in the rishi cult equally sacred to Hindus and Muslims, is only one of the more dramatic manifestations of the Hindu tradition of religious harmony. Tolerating another religion is at best a negative approach, but accepting all religions positively and gladly is a peculiarly Hindu contribution. Its message of the harmony of religions, of the essential unity of mystical experiences, of accepting the divine as so opulent and all-embracing that any effort to move towards it is to be welcomed regardless of its style or idiom, is thus extremely relevant in the modern age.

The Divinity of the Individual

Flowing from the concept of the unity of mankind and the harmony of religions is the third aspect of the Hindu message which reiterates the divinity and dignity of the individual. It is true that Hindu society often appears to be so highly hierarchical and stratified and places so much emphasis upon social duty and status that individual freedom seems to be at a discount. However, it must be remembered that parallel to and, ultimately, overriding these social stratifications runs the basic concept of the divinity of the human individual. Every person born into the human race, regardless of sex or religion, colour or caste, language, or geographical location partakes of the essential mystery of divine potential. Every Atman, in the Hindu view, contains the seeds of spiritual growth and ultimate realisation.

However diverse the circumstances, and however hostile the environment, Hinduism believes that there is within the human psyche the unquenchable spark of divinity that can, sooner or later, be fanned into the blazing fire of spiritual realisation. This concept endows every individual with a dignity that immediately places him, in essence, above and beyond social customs and traditions. Today, when human dignity is at a discount with various collectivities imposing their domination over the individual in a hundred different ways, this aspect of Hinduism's message is of no mean significance. It provides the counterpoint to the concept of human unity, reasserting the unique significance of each individual while stressing the unity of the entire race.

The Quality of Creative Synthesis

The fourth facet of the Hindu ethos flows from its unusual synthesising and syncretising capacity. Against the rigid dichotomy between action in the world and withdrawn meditation, it places the great ideal of the Gita, wherein the way of karma (action) and the way of gyana (knowledge) are fused in the crucible of dedication to the divine; against the cruel dichotomy between matter and energy (which has been breached in the West, not too long ago, by Einstein and his successors), the Indian mind has postulated the essential oneness behind all existence—*isha vasyamidam sarvam yat kincha jagatyam jagat*, the same energy pulsating in the heart of the atom as in the depths of the farthest galaxy—as the *Isha Upanishad* has it; against the dogmatic confrontation between science and religion, there is the vision of both these great disciplines as two different approaches 'towards essentially the same truth, one reaching outwards into the very structure of the cosmos and the other inwards into the very essence of the human psyche. This capacity to balance, to harmonise disparate concepts and apparently contradictory movements, has been the hallmark of the greatest Hindu minds, and carries within it the ideological seeds of a world civilisation in the future which, ideally, would weld together the best traditions of national cultures into a glowing and harmonious synthesis.

Cosmic Values

Finally, in the context of our capacity to break away from the confines of this planet and advance into the vastness of outer space, Hinduism has provided a scheme of cosmic values which are startling in their contemporary relevance. The concept of vast aeons of time through which the world passes (four ages or yugas totalling 4.32 billion years, each adding up to only a single day of Brahma) more closely approximates to the age of this earth than any other scheme of classical calculation. The concept of millions upon millions of galaxies—*koti koti brahmanda*—once considered to be merely an absurd flight of fancy, is now beginning to come alive as the boundless universe unfolds itself before our startled gaze. The vision of the cosmic dance of Shiva, where millions of galaxies spring into being every moment and millions are extinguished in the unending cycle of eternity, reflects the new and evolving knowledge that we are receiving from our initial probing into the universe around us.

And yet, within this incomprehensible vastness, and

perhaps because of it, remains the eternal mystery of the human personality. Among billions of galaxies in the universe, one is ours; among billions of stars in this galaxy, one is ours; among billions of human beings on this planet, is one's individual self, but such is the grandeur and mystery of the Atman that it can move towards a comprehension of the unutterable mystery of existence. We, who are children of the past and the future, of earth and heaven, of light and darkness, of the human and the divine, at once evanescent and eternal, of the world and beyond it, within time and in eternity, yet have the capacity to comprehend our condition, to rise above our terrestrial limitations, and, finally, to transcend the throbbing abyss of space and time itself. This, in essence, is the message of Hinduism.

PART TWO

Essays on Hinduism

FIVE SUTRAS FOR THE GLOBAL SOCIETY, INSPIRED BY VEDANTA

Asia has been the cradle of all the great religions of the world, and has had a rich and varied philosophical heritage coming down unbroken for thousands of years. India, in particular, has been par excellence the nation of multiple religions. Four of the world's great religions were born here—Hinduism, Buddhism, Jainism, and Sikhism; while five have come to us from West Asia and have flourished here for many centuries—Christianity, Judaism, Zoroastrianism, Islam, and the Bahai faith. And there are, of course, several non-formalized indigenous faiths, which are commonly referred to as 'animist' religions, and which predate all our major organized religions.

I am aware that religion is not the same as philosophy, but at least for us in Asia there has always been a close linkage between the two. We do not look upon philosophy—'love of wisdom' in Greek terminology—as merely an intellectual exercise, but rather as a quest for wisdom and enlightenment. It is in this context that I venture to place a set of five sutras, cryptic statements compressing a wealth of meaning, based essentially on the Vedantic philosophy, which between them give us a roadmap for addressing the multiple problems that humanity faces today. In my view, a philosophy is really valid only if it helps us here and now to cope with the multiple challenges of life, otherwise it becomes merely an academic and archival exercise for students and research scholars. For me, philosophy is a vibrant and dynamic exercise that helps us maximize our inner and outer capacities during our life on earth.

The first sutra is from the *Ishavasya Upanishad*: '*Ishavasyamidam Sarvam Yatkinchy Jadatyam Jagat*'—This whole cosmos, not merely the tiny speck of dust that we call planet earth but the billions upon billions of galaxies in the unending universe around us, is illuminated by, inhabited by the same divine power. Whether it is the majestic waltz of the galaxies or the frenetic rock and roll of sub-atomic particles—so powerfully symbolized in the concept of Shiva Nataraja (Lord of the Cosmic Dance)—all owe their existence to the same divine force, or Cosmic Principle, known in the Upanishads as the Brahman. In a way this represents the philosophic correlate of the Unified Field Theory that scientists are looking for to explain all the multiple, mind-boggling phenomena in the cosmos. This gives us a firm foundation to probe deeper into the power that subsumes all that exists, that has and had existed, and that will exist for all time.

Flowing from this is a second sutra from the Bhagavad Gita: *Ishwara Sarbutanam Hriddeshe Tishtati*—The divine power resides in the hearts of all beings. This is tremendously important, because if the divinity was not seated in our hearts there would be no way in which we could approach or experience it. While all creatures have potential divinity, it is only with the emergence of the human race that for the first time there is a species on earth which is self-conscious and which can, therefore, embark on the spiritual quest. Each human being encapsulates a spark of the divine—known as the Atman—and fanning that spark into the blazing fire of spiritual realisation is believed to be the true purpose of human life.

I would like to dwell for a while on the crucial importance of joining the Atman and the Brahman, in other words, raising our consciousness to a radically elevated trans-rational level of awareness. The philosophy and methodology of this joining is what is known as Yoga, which comes from the same root as the English word 'yoke' meaning to join. In our tradition, while there are numerous methodologies to bring about this union, we can recognise four main highways.

The first is what is known as the jnana (or gyana) yoga, the way of wisdom. This involves clarifying and refining the mind so as to be able to discriminate between what is real and what is illusory—*sat-asat viveka*. It could perhaps be compared to the way of Plato who, you will recall, held that all we see are shadows thrown on the wall of the cave in which we are seated; we see neither the objects themselves, far less the light that actually illuminates them. Jnana yoga involves the study of scriptures, meditation, and introspection so that we develop the capacity to perceive the unchanging reality that lies behind all manifestation. The great seers Adi Shankaracharya and Sri Ramana Maharishi are outstanding representations of jnana yoga.

The second main path of yoga is bhakti yoga, the way of devotion. This involves, in effect, falling in love with a personalized figure of the divine, as did the great bhakti saints—from the Nayamars and Alwars in Tamil Nadu to the great Vaishnava devotees Mira Bai, Tulsidas, and Surdas in central India; from Narsi Bhagat in Gujarat to Shankerdeva in Assam, and Sri Chaitnaya in Bengal and Odisha. True bhakti involves a total surrender in love and devotion to one's chosen deity. In the West, it would be comparable to the great Christian devotees like St. Francis of Assissi, St. Theresa of Avila, and St. John on the Cross; and in the Sufi tradition, Jalaluddin Rumi and Amir Khusrau, whose devotion was directed to their gurus, Shams Tabriz and Hazrat Nizamuddin. In India, the bhakti movement had a tremendous impact in moving from the *devavani* (Sanskrit) to the *lokavani* (regional languages), thus taking the message of the Upanishads right to the common person.

The third main path of union with the divine is karma yoga, the yoga of action. The key to this is to be found in the second verse of the *Ishavasyamidam Upanishad,* but it was particularly elaborated by Sri Krishna in the Bhagavad Gita. The concept is that if work is undertaken in a spirit of selfless dedication to the divine, it can also be a powerful vehicle for spiritual realisation. Living as we are in an era when escaping from the world into a mountain retreat is no longer a viable option, and all of us have necessarily to involve ourselves in outer activities, the concept of karma yoga is particularly relevant in this day and age. This was the path chosen by Swami Vivekananda when he set up the Ramakrishna Mission, and was followed by many other such organisations. In the West, this would be the way of Martha, of good work, the way of Mother Teresa, and dedicated Christian missionaries.

If jnana yoga is the way of the mind, bhakti yoga the way of the heart, and karma yoga the way of the hands, then the fourth yoga, known as the raja yoga, is the 'royal path'. This involves becoming aware of and then arousing the spiritual powers inherent in the human body itself. It is believed that a dynamic force known as the kundalini, the serpent power, lies curled three and a half times around the base of the spine. By certain special practices, this power can be aroused so that it travels up the spine, energizing, as it does, a series of seven chakras or plexuses, culminating in the thousand-petalled lotus in the cortex which catapults us into spiritual illumination. While this yoga is mentioned both in the Upanishads and the Gita, it is in the Yoga Sutras of Patanjali that the whole concept is elaborated.

What is now known as Yoga around the world is Hatha Yoga, physical asanas and postures, which in fact represent only a small portion of the raja yoga. Regulation and awareness of our breath, which is the vital link between our body and our consciousness, is the key concept of raja yoga. Sri Aurobindo in his extensive works has shed much light on the higher reaches of consciousness that can be achieved through yoga.

I have mentioned these four paths of yoga simply to highlight the prime importance of joining the Atman and the Brahman in our own lifetime. Vedanta does not postpone illumination until after death; rather, it stresses that we should try and achieve the union here and now. I should also add that these four yogas are not mutually exclusive; each of us can and in fact should try and partake, to some extent, in each one of these paths, concentrating mainly on the one that most appeals to us.

So far, I have covered the first two sutras that I have chosen—the all-pervasive Brahman, the Atman within us, and the four-fold path of Yoga to join the two. Let me now turn to the third important and well-known sutra from the Upanishads which describes the human race as a single family—*Vasudhaiva Kutumbakam.* It is only in our lifetimes that science and technology have actually given us the capacity to break out of the confines of our own Earth, reach the moon and explore the planets and stars beyond. They have given us instant communications, the internet, television, and a vast array of technological instruments which have indeed made the world potentially a single unit. However, it is astonishing that thousands of years ago our seers had realised that, in the final analysis, the human race must be looked upon as a single family. The Upanishads describe the human race as *Amritasya Putraha*, children of immortality. Unfortunately, despite these great concepts and the recent technological breakthroughs, our minds are still mired in pre-global, parochial concepts, and this is the cause of much of the turmoil that we see in the world around us.

If we are ever to move towards a global society, we will have to move beyond our limited nationalisms and realise that in the final analysis we are all inhabitants of a small planet with strictly limited resources that we are rapidly destroying. This is Mother Earth—*Bhawani Vasundhra* in Sanskrit, Gaia in the Greek—which has nurtured consciousness up from the primeval ocean over billions of years to where we are today. Unless we look upon the human race as a single family, we will surely end up destroying both the natural and the human environment. *Vasudhaiva Kutumbakam*, therefore, has to be the key concept of the emerging global society—indeed, of humanity in all ages.

The fourth sutra inspired by Vedanta is from the Rig Veda: *Ekam Sadvipraha Bahudha Vadanti*—the Truth is one, the wise call it by many names. This sutra points out that there are many paths to the divine articulated from time to time and from place to place by great seers, prophets, and avataras. For anyone to assume that there is only one path to the divine is an absurdity. Who are we, creatures on a tiny speck of dust in the universe, to lay down that the illimitable splendour of the Divine can appear only in one form, at one place, and at one time? This is prima facie unacceptable. There are billions of planets in our own galaxy and billions of galaxies in the infinite universe around us. How do we know when and where and in what form the divine force has revealed itself?

On Earth itself, humanity has had numerous and varied experiences of engaging with the Divine, which is why over a dozen great religions flourish around the world. While I can strongly hold that for me my path is the best, I have no right to impose this view on other people and to blow up, decapitate, torture, lynch, intimidate and persecute those who do not follow my path. It is deeply disturbing that such fanaticism and hate-filled violence still exists among us, in all societies, everywhere.

The fifth and the final sutra that I wish to present is *Bahujana Sukhaya, Bahujana Hitaya Cha*—the welfare of the many, the happiness of the many. There is a general misconception that Vedanta involves only a quest for personal salvation without concern for the larger social welfare. In fact, the last three sutras that I have mentioned are directly concerned with the welfare of humanity at large. This one in particular is of great importance, because it stresses that apart from continuing our inner efforts to join the Atman and the Brahman, it is also important that we should be working for the welfare of society.

When Swami Vivekananda founded the Ramakrishna Mission in 1897, he gave them one simple motto: *Aatmano Mokshartham Jagat Hitaya Cha*—work for your inner salvation, but also for the welfare of the world. There have been many definitions of socialism, ranging from Fabian Socialism to Marxism-Leninism, but it seems to me that these five words, *Bahujana Sukhaya, Bahujana Hitaya Cha*, beautifully express the basic ideal that every individual everywhere should be happy. In fact, our prayers are very often dedicated to the general welfare. For example, the famous one:

Sarvepi Sukhina Santu
Sarve Santu Niramaya
Sarve Bhadrani Pashyantu
Ma Kashchit Dukhbhag Bhavet

May all beings be happy,
may all be without disease,
may all perceive auspicious sights,
may no one have to undergo suffering.

While this may be a highly idealistic concept, it shows that Vedanta includes a special emphasis on improving the lot of *every* human being on earth. Indeed, the Vedas go one step further and speak of the welfare of animals, trees, rivers, oceans, mountains, and forests. Clearly, the ancient rishis were aware that we are not separate from each other, and that we are not separate from the entire natural world. In destroying another life, in destroying our environment, we destroy ourselves.

Taken together, these five sutras inspired by the philosophy that, to me, is at the heart of enlightened Hinduism—the unity of all existence, the divinity inherent in each human being and the four-fold path of yoga to join the two, the concept of the human race as a single family, the belief that all religions are ultimately various paths to the same goal, and the commitment to the wider welfare of society and the world—represent a holistic philosophy which is urgently needed at the present, critical juncture of human history.

VEDANTA

The Wisdom of the Upanishads

In this age of turmoil and transition, it sometimes appears as if the human psyche itself is adrift on a vast and turbulent ocean, without any sense of direction, without any landmarks or lighthouses to show the way. There is turmoil in the outer world—there is violence and hatred, killing and suffering all around us; and there is also turmoil in the inner world—the deep psychological currents that rule human consciousness also seem to be disturbed. At a time like this we look towards our great spiritual traditions, not to go back in time, for that is not possible; it is a common mistake for many civilizations to look back in yearning and to long for a so-called 'golden age' that may have existed at one time but which is no longer within the realm of possibility. Within this present space-time continuum, time flows only in one direction and, therefore, there is no advantage in trying to recapture the outer structures of a bygone age. But there is great importance in trying to understand the inner spirit of a tradition.

What is the inner spirit of Hinduism, where does it lie? I believe that it lies in the Vedas. The Vedas stand in all their majesty—like the mighty Himalayas—as the very source and bedrock of Hindu civilization. The Vedas are the inspired utterances of a whole galaxy of realized souls, of spiritual geniuses, of people well versed intellectually but with spiritual enlightenment as well. The Vedas are unique, both because of the timespan over which they were composed—the whole Vedic tradition which has come down to us must have been composed over a period of at least 1000 to 1500 years—and because of the scope and diversity of the people who received these great spiritual messages. And if you look upon the Vedas as the Himalayas of our cultural traditions, the Upanishads can well be described as those great peaks which are so prominent when you view the Himalayas from the air. The peaks are only a part of the entire mountain range, and yet it is they, with the eternal snow upon them, that draw our minds and our admiration.

The Upanishads are known as the Vedanta—'the end of the Vedas'—both because chronologically they come at the end of the Vedas, and also because philosophically they represent the highest watermark, the culmination of the Vedic civilization and genius. One meaning of the word Upanishad is 'to sit nearby'. In the Indian tradition, the guru would be seated under a tree, near a river or a lake, and one or more disciples would cluster around him to learn the eternal wisdom. This is interesting, because it is in juxtaposition to the Greek tradition where Socrates and his disciples, including

Plato, would not sit but walk up and down the corridors of their academy. In all other aspects, however, the Socratic dialogues and the Upanishads have a great deal in common; they are all dialogues between the guru and shishya.

In Sanskrit, a single word or phrase can have many shades of meaning, and they are not mutually exclusive. We do not accept the rigid dyarchy whereby one word can have only one meaning. Another meaning of Upanishad is the 'secret doctrine'. In the *Mundaka Upanishad* the great householder Shaunaka goes to the sage Angiras and asks him the famous question: '*Kasmin nu bhagavo vijnyate sarvam idam vijnyatatan bhavati iti?* (Venerable sir, what is that by knowing which everything becomes known)?' And in reply to that question the teacher expounds the theory of the two types of knowledge, the higher and the lower, the *parividya* and the *aparividya.*

The Upanishads deal with the higher knowledge, which is suprarational knowledge. It does not negate rationality, it transcends it, because, while the mind is a brilliant and multifaceted instrument, it is nonetheless limited by its very structure. There are ranges of knowledge and experience which do not come within the ambit of so-called rational thinking. At some point in our adventure of consciousness the mind has to be transcended, and the Upanishads deal with the higher knowledge, the suprarational realization which comes not by intellectual gymnastics but by spiritual realization. The ultimate goal of knowledge, spiritual realization, is the basis of all Upanishadic teaching.

Again, in the *Mundaka*, there are two memorable verses

which describe what the Upanishads are really supposed to do. They are likened to a great bow upon which the arrow must be fastened, sharpened by meditation and *sadhana*. The arrow is the Atman; the target is the Brahman and the bow is Aum, the sacred word. The bow has to be drawn with great attention and single-mindedness, only then do we become one with the Brahman in the same way as an arrow becomes one with its target. That is the central point of the teaching, and the Upanishads are the vehicle for this merger of the Atman and the Brahman—or, in theological terms, the soul becoming one with god. This is an approximate translation, of course, for the words 'god' and 'soul' are not really part of the Vedantic tradition, and have certain connotations in the Semitic religions which are not entirely parallel to Hinduism.

Traditionally, there are said to be 108 Upanishads, which is a sacred number. But the major Upanishads number about fourteen. Adi Shankaracharya wrote his luminous commentaries upon eleven of these Upanishads: the *Isha*, the *Kena*, the *Katha*, the *Prashna*, the *Mundaka*, the *Mandukya*, the *Aitareya*, the *Taittiriya*, the *Chandogya*, the *Brihadaranyaka*, and the *Svetashvatara*. The texts vary considerably in length. The *Isha Upanishad*, for example, has only eighteen mantras, whereas the *Brihadaranyaka*, the Upanishad of the great forest, runs into many hundreds of verses. Despite their diversity and the fact that they were composed over a vast period of time, there is an inner unity among the Upanishads which is quite extraordinary. All of the great seers seem to be talking about the same basic experience, that is, the experience of the

Divine, of the Brahman. So, the Upanishads can be said to be essentially the Gyana-marga, the way of knowledge, and for that there are only two qualifications laid down for the teacher: he must be *srotriya* and *brahmanishtha*, well versed in the scriptures but also founded upon spiritual realization. It is important to remember that the Upanishadic teaching is not a mere academic exercise; it is a teaching for spiritual quest.

The cardinal concepts of the Upanishads can be briefly listed as five.

The first and most basic concept can perhaps be expressed in a line explaining the all-pervasive Brahman: *isa vasyam idam sarvam yat kinca jagatyam jagat* (Whatever exists and wherever it exists is permeated by the same divine power and force). This is an important realization, because many philosophies have postulated dichotomies between God and the world, between matter and spirit, between good and evil, between the divine and the devil, and so on. But the Upanishadic view is that in the ultimate analysis all that exists is a manifestation of the divine. Indeed, there can be no manifestation without divinity behind it, and this, in a way, is the realization of the new science. Previously, in the classical science of Newton, there was the dichotomy between matter and spirit, matter and energy; but post-Einstein you find a realization that whatever exists is really the same energy. It may appear as matter, it may appear as energy; it may appear as a particle or as a wave, but it is essentially the same energy. So, the unified-force theory towards which the scientists are desperately probing has its spiritual counterpart in the concept of the all-pervasive

Brahman of the Upanishads. The greatest realization is to see the Brahman everywhere, wherever you look above or below, to the right or to the left, within or without. This is the first important concept of Vedantic knowledge.

The second concept is that this Brahman resides within each individual consciousness, in the Atman. The Atman, as it were, is the reflection of this all-pervasive Brahman in individual consciousness; but the Atman is not ultimately separate from the Brahman, it is a reflection of that Brahman, it is a part of it. One of the examples given in the Upanishads is that as, when a great fire is lighted, millions of sparks fly up out of the fire and then fall back into it, so from the Brahman arise all these millions of galaxies and into Brahman again they all ultimately disappear. The concept of *isvarah sarvabhutanam hriddese 'rjuna tishthati*, of the Lord residing within the heart of each individual, is the second great insight of the Upanishads, and the relationship between the Atman and the Brahman is the basis upon which Vedantic teaching revolves. All the four yogas are directed towards bringing about the union between the Atman and the Brahman. Yoga is that which joins the Atman and the Brahman. There are in our tradition four major paths of yoga: gyana yoga, the way of wisdom; bhakti yoga, the way of emotional rapport; karma yoga, the way of dedicated action; and raja yoga, the way of psychic discipline. All of them are directed towards bringing about the union between the all-pervasive Brahman without and the immortal Atman within.

Flowing from this, we now come to the third important

Vedantic concept: that all human beings, because of their shared spirituality, are members of a single, extended family. The Upanishads have an extraordinary phrase for human beings, *amritasya putrah* (children of immortality). We do not look upon human beings as essentially sinners, weak, and begging some unseen being hidden in some seventh heaven. Rather, we are children of immortality, because we carry the light and the power of the Brahman within our consciousness. This is within the consciousness of every human being regardless of race or colour, creed or sex, or any other differentiation. That is the basis of the concept of human beings as an extended family: *Vasudhaiva kutumbakam*. A famous shloka, not from the Upanishads but from a later text, points out that making a distinction between 'mine' and 'yours' is the small and narrow way of looking at reality, indulged in by people with small minds. But for those of the greater consciousness, the entire world is a family. This is another great insight of the Upanishad.

The fourth major philosophical concept of the Upanishads is the essential unity of all religions, of all spiritual paths—*ekam sad viprah bahudha vadanti* (Truth is one, the wise call it by many names) as mentioned in the Rig Veda. The *Mundaka Upanishad* has a beautiful mantra which says that as streams and rivulets arise in different parts of the world but ultimately flow into the same ocean, so do all the various creeds and religious formulations arise in different times and areas, but, if they have true aspiration, they ultimately reach the same goal.

Here is a philosophy which cuts across barriers of hatred

and fanaticism that have been built in the name of religion. The Vedanta is a universal religion; it accepts the infinite possibilities of movements towards the divine, it does not seek to limit or confine us to any particular formulation. After all, each one of us is different. Whether you believe in reincarnation or in genetic configuration, the fact remains that there are no two human beings who are exactly alike, and so all have to seek their own path to the divine. The Vedanta welcomes and accepts the multiplicity of paths to the divine, provided those paths are true paths towards divine realization, not merely intellectual gymnastics and disputations. It is a little like climbing a mountain. There are several different starting points, and if we keep arguing at those starting points we are miles apart. But when we start climbing and are actually moving upwards then, as we come nearer and nearer to the summit, our paths will begin to converge and ultimately when we get to the top we will all meet there. Similarly, once you really start moving upwards in the field of spiritual endeavour, you will find these denominational differences gradually losing their importance, and as you rise to the summit you will realize the spiritual oneness of divinity.

The fifth Vedantic concept is the welfare of all beings: *Bahujana sukhaya bahujana hitaya cha*. The Vedanta does not seek to throw one class against another class, one caste against another caste, or one group against another group. The Vedanta seeks the welfare of all creation, not only of human beings but also of what we call the lower creatures. In our arrogance we have destroyed the environment of this planet, we have polluted the oceans, we have made the air unbreathable, we have desecrated nature and decimated wildlife. So many species have become extinct because of our *ahamkara (arrogance)* as human beings. But the Vedantic seers knew that man was not something apart from nature, that human consciousness grew out of the entirety of the world situation and, therefore, they had compassion for all living beings. That is why the Vedanta constantly exhorts that, while we are working for our own salvation, we must also shun the path of violence, shun the path of hatred, and try and develop both elements of inner and outer work: *Atmano mokshartham jagat hitaya cha*. Indeed, these are two sides of the same coin; we must work for our own salvation, and also for the welfare of the world. We also have a social responsibility, and as long as we are embodied, we have to continue to work for the welfare of all beings.

These five concepts from the Vedanta—the all-pervasive Brahman; the Atman which resides in all beings; the concept of the human race as members of a family regardless of all differences; the idea that all religions are essentially different paths to the same goal; and the concept that we must work for the welfare of society as a whole and for the welfare of this entire ecosystem and not only for ourselves—if taken together, these concepts provide us a comprehensive world-view that will greatly help us in our troubled times.

We are living in a very difficult age, but it is also an exciting age to be alive in, particularly for the younger generations. People today are often upset and worried as to why everything is so turbulent, but that is inevitable, because we are in a period of major transition. It is my belief, strengthened over the last few decades by travelling extensively throughout the world, that mankind today is at a transition as important as those in the past—from nomadic to pastoral civilization, then from pastoral to agricultural, agricultural to industrial, and to post-industrial civilization. Each transition is now coming quicker because of the accelerated pace of growth and development, and what is happening is that a global consciousness is beginning to emerge despite all our discords and problems. There are many setbacks, of course, and sometimes we appear to be regressing, sliding back into darkness, and creating divisions that we seemed to have overcome; but these are aberrations, and the larger trend is of overcoming the many divisions of the past.

We are too close to events to really grasp what is happening, but I see a paradigm shift. Gradually, a new world civilization is being born. And it *has* to be born if mankind is to survive in and beyond the 21st century. Science and technology have given us tremendous power, but that power can be used for benign or malignant purposes. We can abolish poverty and hunger, malnutrition and misery, illiteracy, and unemployment from the face of this earth. It can be done quite easily—just a few days' expenditure diverted from world armaments, for instance, is enough to abolish hunger on the planet. But, instead, thousands of billions of dollars, roubles, pounds, and rupees, and other currencies, are going into the manufacture of weapons of destruction every year. We must never forget that power by itself is neither good nor evil; there is the *daivi shakti* and there is the *asuri shakti*—the benign power and the malignant power. The worship of power, of science, is not enough. Hitler's gas chambers were an example of science and technology; the Hiroshima and Nagasaki atom bombs were also an example of science and technology. In the many decades since, science has given us means to perpetrate far greater horrors—or do far greater good to all humanity, indeed, to the planet, than was ever possible.

At this time, as in any other, we can survive only if we have an alternative ideology to the present one that has led mankind to this position. The Vedanta, in fact, provides such an alternative ideology. In the *Shvetashvatara Upanishad* the seer says: *Vedaham etam purusham mahantam aditya varnam tamasah parstat* (I know that great being, shining like the sun beyond the darkness; it is only by such knowing that you can overcome death, there is no other way to immortality). The immortality of the Upanishads is not survival after death, that is already taken for granted, it is the transcending of birth and death. The immortality of the Upanishads means that our consciousness is raised to a state where we are not obliged to be born and reborn again and again in the cycle of *samsara*, the mortal, material world. In the Buddhist tradition we have the bodhisattvas who had attained 'Buddhahood' but turned back in order to help suffering humanity. In the Upanishadic tradition we have the *siddhas*, people who materialize anywhere at will in order to help humanity.

So, it is not a question of being selfish but of being able to break the bonds in which we are caught. Can you imagine what it is like when a caterpillar, a land-bound worm, goes into a chrysalis and a miraculous metamorphosis takes place so that it emerges as a beautiful, radiantly coloured butterfly? That is the sort of metamorphosis the Upanishads envisage for human consciousness. We change from our earth-bound consciousness into this bright, multi-coloured consciousness which can still alight upon the ground like a caterpillar but can also fly into the air which the caterpillar could not. That, as I see it, is the true message of the Upanishads, seen in that great and immortal Vedic prayer that seeks to lead us from the untruth of ignorance into the truth of knowledge; from the darkness within us into the light above us, and from the cycle of birth and death into immortality:

Asato ma sad gamaya!
Tamaso ma jyotir gamaya!
Mrityor ma amytam gamaya!

That is the highest achievement of the Upanishads; and that is the goal towards which we all must strive.

YOGA

An Integrated Philosophy of Life

Yoga represents a central and pivotal concept in Indian culture, and some understanding of this is essential for those who wish to grasp the deeper significance behind Hinduism. The relationship between the Brahman and the Atman, between the all-pervasive divinity and its reflection within individual consciousness, is the main concept behind Vedantic philosophy. Spiritual realization involves in some way a joining of the Atman and the Brahman in its broadest sense. Yoga represents both the process as well as the goal of this union. It brings experiential and holistic dimensions into religious quest, without which the whole exercise remains one of intellectual disputation without any real spiritual progress.

Theoretically, there can be an infinite number of different ways to approach the divine; indeed, as many paths as there are individuals. However, in the Hindu tradition, these approaches can largely be said to fall into four major categories gyana yoga, bhakti yoga, karma yoga and raja yoga. While the path is essentially an integrated one, each yoga lays special emphasis upon different human faculties.

Let us start with gyana yoga, the yoga of wisdom or intellectual discrimination. This is a path particularly suited for those whose intellects are highly developed. The discipline consists of developing the ability to discriminate between the real and the unreal, the ephemeral and the eternal, until finally spiritual realization is achieved. The classical texts of the gyana yoga are the Upanishads, which are based on the collective realization of a whole galaxy of realized seers or rishis over at least a thousand years. They present in memorable language the great Vedantic truths which stand behind the tradition of gyana yoga.

While the Upanishads have been the spiritual source for all the schools of Indian philosophy, it is Adi Shankara, the great 8th century reformer and exponent of monism, with whom the gyana-marga is specially associated. He interpreted Vedanta, as leading to Brahma-gyana or knowledge of the Absolute. It is to his glowing commentaries on the Upanishads, the Brahma-Sutras and the Bhagavad Gita that we owe a great deal of our understanding of this path. The gyana yoga can perhaps be compared to the wisdom of Solomon, or to the great Socratic dialogues so beautifully recorded by Plato. In this path, it is the intellect that has to be increasingly illuminated by the divine truth, so that ultimately it is transcended when spiritual realization is achieved.

While gyana yoga deals essentially with the intellect, bhakti yoga is based upon a spiritualizing of the other great human faculty, that of the emotions. The mind and the heart are two predominant aspects of the human personality, and if the gyana yoga revolves around a progressive spiritualizing of the mind, the bhakti yoga does the same for the emotions. The concept that the emotions are a hindrance to the spiritual path is not justified. They certainly can be, if they are misdirected or undisciplined; but when directed towards the divine they can be a potent source of spiritual realization.

Bhakti yoga involves the turning of the emotions towards the divine envisaged in a human form, whether it is Shiva or Vishnu, Rama or Krishna, the goddess or Subrahmanya, or any other. It involves the passionate outpouring of the emotions, culminating in a spiritual rapture of union with the chosen divine form, and is, therefore, characteristic of theism, with its emphasis on personal divinity, surrender, and grace. The history of all religions is replete with instances of such devotion. Sri Chaitanya who was born more than 500 years ago, re-established the great cult of Krishna worship throughout the country, while Sri Ramakrishna worshipped the goddess Kali as the divine mother. South India has produced a whole series of saints devoted to Shiva and Vishnu. In the Christian tradition, we have saints like St. Theresa of Avila, St. John of the Cross, St. Francis of Assisi and many others. In Hinduism, there are numerous texts on bhakti yoga, predominant of which is the *Srimad Bhagavatam* which deals with the incarnation of Vishnu, especially as Krishna, the Shiva Purana, and the Shaiva texts of south India. The great mystic poetry of medieval India represents the anguish and ecstasy of the bhakta in a most lyrical and profound way.

Karma yoga is the way of right action. In the Bhagavad Gita, one of the greatest religious texts of the world, the theory of karma is expounded to encompass all actions done as an offering to the divine. *Yogah karmasu kausalam* (Yoga is skill in actions), says Krishna to Arjuna on the battlefield of life, and adds: 'Thou hast the right only to the deeds, not to the fruit thereof.'

The theory of karma yoga is complex and subtle. We all have to work, not only for our sheer material existence but also for our intellectual and emotional welfare. But if all action is bondage, as some philosophers seem to claim, then it would appear that we are all doomed to eternal suffering on the constantly revolving wheel of *samsara*. However, Krishna points out that it is not the action itself which is the cause of bondage, but rather the psychological attitude behind that action. Therefore, if action is done as an offering to the divine, if it is performed with devotion and dedication, but without an obsessive attachment to its consequences, then that action itself becomes a potent instrument for spiritual development. Indeed, Krishna expressly points out in the Gita that many persons, including the great King Janaka, achieved realization through karma yoga. Perhaps Kant's ethical standpoint in the West may, to some degree, correspond with this view of action.

The Bhagavad Gita is considered to be the prime text for karma-yoga, although it deals with all the four yogas, and, as Sri Aurobindo points out in his glowing *Essays on the Gita*, it presents before us an integrated philosophy of life. In the Western tradition, it can be said that the Christian denominations which have specially taken upon themselves the work of spreading education and medical services throughout the world are in the tradition of the Karma yoga. Several Christian and other groups exist today, who dedicate their lives to service and the alleviation of suffering, both physical and psychic. Mother Teresa is an unparalleled example of this Christian commitment of service to suffering humanity as a dedication to the divine.

We come now to the fourth path which is known as raja-yoga, the royal path. Whether this term is used because the path is considered to be particularly effective, or because it was, in fact, preferred by the ruling classes in ancient India, is a debatable point. It is true, however, that this is in some ways the most potent and dramatic way of achieving union between the human and the divine. It revolves around techniques to modify our normal waking consciousness and thereby bring about a dramatic encounter with the unlimited power of the divine. It is here that Patanjali's Yoga-Sutras have such an important role to play.

Because the yogic asanas involve manipulation of the body, an erroneous impression seems to be prevalent that yoga is simply some kind of complicated physical exercises. This is a very restricted view of yoga. While certainly yoga asanas can have a dramatic impact upon our bodily condition and can significantly improve our general health, it would be wrong to limit their effects only to the body. It can be recalled that Patanjali's eight steps start with *yamas* and *niyamas*, which involve certain psychological restraints and disciplines, and bring in asanas, pranayama, and pratyahara only as the third, fourth, and fifth steps. The remaining three steps again are essentially psychological. We must always remember, therefore, that yoga is very much more than simply the capacity to perform difficult physical postures. Indeed, the interior or *antaranga*-yoga is the more significant achievement when compared to the outer, the *bahiranga* aspects.

Another point needs to be made, and that relates to the whole question of the kundalini and its awakening. The yoga tradition postulates the existence of a divine power—the kundalini—located at the base of the spine and often called the serpent power, because it is coiled like a snake three and a half times when at rest. Under certain conditions, and by various practices including asanas and pranayama, regulation of the breathing process, it is possible to stimulate this kundalini into movement. When it uncoils and starts rising, it progressively penetrates seven chakras or centres along the spinal system until it finally bursts in ecstasy into the thousand-petalled lotus in the cerebral cortex and the yogi is flooded with the *Brahma-samsparsa*, the contact with the Brahman.

A whole science, known as the Tantra, has developed around the kundalini-yoga. After Patanjali's seminal work there have been many other texts in the Hindu and Buddhist traditions, as well as commentaries upon them. A century ago, a remarkable Englishman, Sir John Woodroffe, wrote a series of pioneering books on various Tantric texts under the pseudonym of Arthur Avalon, and in our own times Pandit Gopi Krishna, whom I last met in Switzerland in 1979, has written a memorable series of books on this astounding phenomenon. This is an aspect that must be kept in mind by all serious practitioners of yoga, so that if the kundalini starts moving they are prepared to absorb the experience in a positive and creative manner. This is a matter with which the guru has to deal because of its tremendous potential both for progress and, if mishandled, for disaster.

While on this question of raja yoga and changed states of consciousness, it needs to be pointed out that, with all its aberrations, the drug phenomenon, specially Lysergic acid diethylamide (LSD), has opened the minds of many in the West who previously had decisively dismissed the whole kundalini phenomenon as either a fraud or a self-imposed hallucination. The work of Stanislav Grof on LSD therapy, and the amazing series of books by Carlos Castaneda, are only two of the numerous indications that the conceptual revolution, begun by Aldous Huxley in his small but seminal book *The Doors of Perception* (1954), has, in fact, gathered tremendous momentum and shows no signs of declining. The gross misuse and exploitation of drugs, which has become an international menace, has most unfortunately distorted the possibility of their creative use by serious spiritual teachers as a trigger to break into higher states of consciousness. Of course, this issue is still very controversial—and the discipline required to achieve psychic wholeness without the use of external stimuli is still far more desirable. Carl Gustav Jung, with his tremendous insights in this field, has contributed enormously to the knowledge of the self in the modern context.

I have broadly described the four major paths to the divine—the path of wisdom, the path of devotion, the path of dedicated action and the path of psychic discipline. These four can, in fact, be combined into an integrated philosophy of life. Humankind today is living in a unique situation. Science and technology are transforming human civilization before our very eyes, and in our own lifetimes we have witnessed incredible breakthroughs in numerous fields. Agriculture, industry, medicine, and communications, all have benefited tremendously from the efflorescence of human creativity expressed through science and technology. And yet the destructive potential of humankind also grows apace—tens of thousands of nuclear weapons of such potency exist that can destroy not only the human race but probably all life on this planet. This is the dilemma of man in the nuclear age.

At such a juncture we can no longer be content with following a single path; what is needed is an integrated, multifaceted endeavour. We need the mind to be illuminated by gyana (wisdom); the heart to be flooded by bhakti (devotion); the will to be disciplined by karma (action); and the psyche to be spiritualized by raja (practice). It is only if we are able to develop all these four elements of our personality that we will achieve the capacity to function as integrated and harmonious human beings, capable of building a new, global civilization on planet earth. And, surely, we can today accept no lesser goal than to be pioneers of the global consciousness that is painfully struggling to be born on our beautiful planet, on Mother Earth that has nurtured the human race up from the slime of the primeval ocean to where we stand today, poised on the threshold of a new leap forward.

SHIVA

Lord of the Cosmic Dance

Know him to be the supreme pervader,
In whom the whole universe is smaller
Than the smallest atom. May he, Shiva,
Fill our heart with infinite peace.
Know him to be the supreme guardian
Of the cosmos, protecting all creatures
From within. May he, Shiva, in whom all
Are one, free us from the bonds of death.

—*Shvetashvatara Upanishad*
(Translation by Eknath Easwaran)

***

At the still point of the turning world. Neither flesh nor fleshless;
Neither from nor towards; at the still point, there the dance is,
But neither arrest nor movement. And do not call it fixity,
Where past and future are gathered. Neither movement from nor towards,
Neither ascent nor decline. Except for the point, the still point,
*There would be no dance, and there is only the dance.**

—T.S. Eliot, *Four Quartets*

* These lines from 'Burnt Norton', the first poem of *Four Quartets*, are widely believed to be inspired by Shiva as Nataraja, the lord of dance.

In our end (to paraphrase T.S. Eliot) is our beginning, for the Cosmos is eternal; creation culminates in dissolution only to emerge from it again. This timeless Cosmic Dance is the dance of Shiva. Indeed, it *is* Shiva. He is both death and life, nought and infinity.

Shiva is surely the most fascinating, enigmatic, powerful, and resplendent of all gods in the Hindu pantheon. There are several reasons for this. The first is his antiquity. Whereas the Vishnu avataras, Rama and Krishna, were born and passed away in historical time, Shiva was neither born nor will he ever pass away. He first appears, appropriately enough, as a pillar of light. The story goes that Brahma and Vishnu were arguing with each other as to who was superior when suddenly a massive pillar of light appeared, which stunned the two gods. They tried to find out where it began and where it ended. Brahma, riding on his Hansa, the swan, flew upwards while Vishnu in the form of Varaha, the boar, went downwards, but neither of them could find the beginning or the end of this great pillar. When they returned, Shiva made himself manifest, clearly reflecting his superiority. But Brahma would not accept defeat and lied that he had reached the top of the pillar of light. As a result, Shiva cursed him that he would not be worshipped anywhere, while Vishnu, who accepted that he had been humbled, was blessed that he would be worshipped along with Shiva himself. This, it is said, is one of the reasons why Brahma is not worshipped in Hindu homes while the worship of Vishnu is a parallel stream of devotion with that of Shiva.

Even historically, in the context of religious belief, Shiva predates every other major deity of Hinduism worshipped today. His origins go back to the pre-Vedic era. There is an image among the seals of the Harappan Civilization which is clearly recognizable as Shiva, or Pashupati, lord of the animals—a figure sitting cross-legged like a yogi, wearing a headgear with horns and surrounded by several animal figures, among them a tiger, an elephant, a buffalo, and a rhinoceros. Some scholars date the Shiva image and concept to a much earlier period, linking it to the Bhimbetka cave paintings of 10,000 BC which show a dancing figure with a trident. In fact, there is reason to believe that Shiva has strong Adivasi roots because he is believed to have first appeared in Mount Kailasha, which was always part of India's cultural geography but beyond the Aryan heartland and inhabited by powerful tribes. Among his numerous names is Kirata, a term used in early Sanskrit literature for non-Aryan people of the eastern Himalayas. Also, he is bare-bodied but for a piece of tiger-skin, and he has been depicted in different eras holding the weapons of a hunter—club, spear, axe, and bow-and-arrow.

In post-Harappan history, Shiva first appears in the Rig Veda (composed between 1500 and 1000 BC) as the storm god Rudra, the 'howler'. He is a figure of fear, wild and unpredictable, but also a healer associated with herbs and poisons. He lives on the fringes of Aryan society among long-haired ascetics who are 'clothed in wind', in other words, naked, and imbibe intoxicants. Rudra-Shiva was thus the outsider who could not be included in Vedic rituals like the fire sacrifice, or yagna, conducted by the Aryan priests.

It would appear that the orthodox Hindu Brahmanical structure was well established by the time of the Puranas (roughly from the third to the AD 7th century . This involved a rigid caste structure whereby four major castes were clearly delineated: the Brahmins (priests), the Kshatriyas (warriors), the Vaishyas (traders), and the Shudras (working class). Beyond the pale of these four were the 'outcastes', whose maltreatment is a stigma on the whole structure of Hindu civilization, much as the entire Greek civilization with all its glory was essentially based on the abominable system of slavery. The Brahmins were at first deeply troubled by this outsider, Shiva, who lived among 'outcaste' tribal people unschooled and uninterested in the traditional Hindu structure, and had his own eating, drinking, and smoking habits, some of which were anathema to the orthodox. He was beyond ideas of 'purity' and 'impurity', he had no time for wealth, status, or family. Indeed, it took a long while for Shiva to be accepted into the orthodox Hindu fold. However, his powers were so great, his persona so vital and compelling, that ultimately they were unable to reject him. This is clearly brought out in the story of the mighty sage Daksha Prajapati.

But before that, let us look at the story of Uma, or Sati, Daksha's daughter. It was her determined love for Shiva that eventually made a passionate lover and householder of the ascetic whose refusal to be bound by desire was so extreme that he had burnt the god of love, Kamadeva, to ashes. Uma was in fact Mahadevi or Shakti, the primordial goddess, who had taken human form in order to unite with Shiva and thus make him complete. When she was very young, she left her father's palace for the forest, where she lived as a hermit practicing great austerities, until Shiva was forced to relent and agree to marry her.

Daksha Prajapati—believed to be one of the sons of Brahma—was a powerful figure, a great king who formulated the rules of Vedic society and ensured the survival of the traditional order. He followed the rituals laid down in the religious texts strictly and expected everyone to do the same. Although details about his family vary in different legends and texts, according to most he had twenty-four daughters, the fifteenth of whom was Uma, who was also his favourite. When she developed an intense love for Shiva, Daksha was aghast because he looked upon Shiva as an outcast who not only defied sacred rituals but had also once insulted Daksha by not bowing to him. However, he had to give in to his daughter's wish and reluctantly agree to her marriage with Shiva, but he was left furious. Sometime later, Daksha organized a great yagna to which all the gods and demigods were invited except Shiva. When Uma heard of this, she insisted that she would go, despite Shiva's objections. When she reached the hall where the yagna was to take place, no one rose to greet her and her father spoke piercing words: 'You were not invited, why did you come? Have you had enough of your vagabond husband?' Uma then realized that the ceremony was an elaborate ritual aimed at insulting her husband. Unable to bear the humiliation, she immolated herself.

When Shiva learnt of Uma's death he was consumed

with grief and rage. Plucking a single hair from his head he dashed it on the ground and a terrible being, Virabhadra, emerged. Shiva asked him to destroy the sacrifice, and the resulting carnage is too terrible to describe. Daksha himself was beheaded and his severed head tossed into the sacrificial fire. Then Shiva stormed into the hall. The survivors of the carnage fell at his feet and begged for mercy. He was, after all, the god who is as compassionate as he is terrifying. His anger abated, and instantly a fragrant breeze swept across the scene. The dead gods arose as if waking from a slumber. Shiva found the headless body of Daksha and brought it back to life, replacing his head with that of a goat. He also gifted Daksha the city of Bhogya, of uninhibited pleasure, which he had originally created for Uma. Daksha was overwhelmed by Shiva's generosity and began to sing his praises. Now Daksha completed his sacrifice, this time giving Shiva his rightful share. This terrible event marked the realization by the orthodox priests that Shiva could no longer be kept out of their worship. Thus, Shiva ceased to be an outcast and outsider. He was accepted, adorned and finally became part of the celestial pantheon. Interestingly, to this day Shiva is always invoked at the end of a pooja with the words 'Har Har Mahadev' accompanied by the raising of both hands, which is a universal gesture of surrender.

However, Uma was dead and Shiva was feeling intense pain. After the yagna, he picked up the lifeless body and walked out of the sacrificial hall. Distraught, he wandered across the world with Uma's corpse in his arms, tears rolling down his cheeks. Brahma and Vishnu were deeply disturbed and realized that if this did not stop, the whole cosmos would be submerged in Shiva's agony. Vishnu then spun his mighty discus—the sudarshan chakra—and it cut Uma's corpse into a hundred pieces. The spots where these fell came to be regarded as Shakti Peeths, centres of goddess worship. Shiva then retired into the icy caves of the Himalayas in deep sorrow and became absorbed in yoga, totally cut off from the rest of the world.

However, in India everything is cyclical. Centuries later, the king of the great Himalayas, Himavan, and his wife Mena gave birth to a beautiful daughter known as Parvati, daughter of the mountains. She was Uma, or Sati, reborn, the Mother Goddess herself, and was determined to bring Shiva out of his isolation and make him a householder once again. Every day she went into Shiva's cave with gifts of fruits and flowers, swept the floor and tended the fire, until Shiva finally agreed to marry her.

There are delightful descriptions of Shiva's baraat, or wedding procession, in popular legend and folk songs and paintings. Along with Brahma and Vishnu and lesser gods and demigods, there were also strange and frightening demons, ghosts and goblins in the procession. Shiva himself, high on bhang (cannabis), had smeared his body with ash and had serpents round his neck. Apparently, Parvati's relatives were terrified and her mother fainted at the sight of the groom and his companions!

Shiva's baraat is wonderful proof of his unconventional persona, his earthy nature and remarkable inclusiveness. It also proves how immense were his powers and his appeal. He broke all the rules of traditional religion and yet became perhaps the greatest god of Hinduism.

***

After the Vedic gods—Indra, Varuna, Agni, Vayu, and others—retired into the background, the Hindu trinity of Brahma, Vishnu, and Shiva emerged as the predominant feature in classical Hinduism. Brahma, who is seated on a lotus that emerged from Vishnu's navel, is the creator, Vishnu himself is the protector and Shiva is the regenerator, the one who destroys old structures so that new beginnings can be made. It is interesting to note that of the trinity, it is Shiva alone who is believed to live on earth, on Mount Kailasha. Brahma is in Brahma Loka, Vishnu in Vaikuntha, but Shiva made his home among us mortals. Also, he is the only one who married a human being, Uma/Parvati. In a way, therefore, he resonates more deeply with the common people. Despite his rather forbidding accoutrements he is of surpassing beauty—Sundereshwara; despite his fearsome aspects, he is the embodiment of compassion—Karunavataram; and he is easily pleased—Ashutosha. In fact, the word Shiva itself means auspicious in Sanskrit.

An important aspect of Shiva is that he is *Nikhil Bhaya Haram*, the destroyer of all fears. Everything that is fearful is under his control, so if we worship him, all fears disappear. We are afraid of death—he is Mahakaleshwara, the great Lord of Death; we are afraid of ghosts—he is Bhooteshwara, Lord of the Ghosts; we are afraid of snakes—he wears the great serpent round his neck; we are afraid of fire—he carries it in one hand as he dances; we are afraid of water—the Ganga sprouts from his locks; we are afraid of illness—he is Vaidyanatha, the great healer, and so on.

Another aspect of Shiva is that he transcends the opposites which we take for granted. For example, on the one hand he is an ascetic sitting alone on Mount Kailasha, lost in deep meditation, on the other hand he is a passionate husband to Parvati and a family man with two children, Ganesha and Kartikeya. Again, he and Parvati represent the masculine and feminine qualities which ultimately merge in the remarkable bi-sexual sculpture of Ardhanarishvara (half man and half woman), thus transcending the sexual polarities that we usually take for granted.

Significantly, Shiva is the only god who is worshiped both by the Devas and the Asuras; the divine forces and the titanic ones. Constantly at war with each other, the Devas and Asuras both feel obliged to bow before Shiva and take his blessings. The Puranas tell us that the Asuras with all their unseemly shapes and bizarre actions insisted on joining Shiva's wedding procession when he was on his way to wed Parvati, to which Shiva readily agreed. Similarly, there are no caste restrictions as far as Shiva is concerned. All who are excluded from society find their refuge in him. He also transcends the dichotomy between what we would normally call good and evil, positive and negative forces, thereby representing an integrated divinity. He is described as *tejomayam, sadunirgunam, adwityam, anandakandam aparajitam aprameyam*—resplendent, with form and formless, unique, the abode of bliss, the unconquerable, the immeasurable.

***

Unlike in most other religions, our gods are fond of music and love to dance. Krishna had his famous dances with the gopis whose mellow and romantic tunes were in keeping with the magical ambience of rural Vrindavan. In sharp contradistinction is the cosmic dance of Shiva—the Tandava—which includes creation, preservation, destruction, regeneration and is accompanied by powerful sound and movement. It is the representation of all existence, because everything is always moving. The galaxies are moving just as the subatomic particles are moving and our consciousness is forming and reforming. Shiva's Tandava has two moods. At a time of destruction, he dances the Vinasha (or Rudra) Tandava, which represents the annihilation of the universe, and when he is in a joyful and creative mood, he dances the Ananda Tandava and the ripples of his bliss spread across all creation.

The dance of Shiva is beautifully captured in what is the high watermark of Hindu art—the image of Nataraja, Lord of the Cosmic Dance. Here, the creativity of Indian sculpture is at its zenith. It is interesting to contrast the Nataraja with the equally creative figure of the Buddha in quiet contemplation. Indeed, these could be looked upon as the two poles of Indian sculpture, the kinetic Nataraja and the still Buddha, both images which have been the focus of intense devotion for millions around the world for many centuries.

The Nataraja image is rich with symbolism. The nimbus of fire surrounding the Dancer represents the all-pervading cosmos. Shiva's right hand holds a small drum, the damaru, which represents the primal sound from which the universe springs. His left hand holds the fire into which ultimately all creation has to fall. Had there been only these two arms there would be no place for humanity. Therefore, his third arm has an upraised palm which is saying, 'Do Not Fear', while the fourth arm points to his raised foot as the road to liberation. He dances on a small human form which represents our ego that needs to be suppressed but not killed. One of his ears sports a male earring, while in the other ear there is a female earring, again representing the fusion of male and female powers. His hair flowing outwards as a result of his dance is cosmic energy, and on his head there is the crescent moon which represents the waxing and waning of Time.

There are numerous interpretations of Nataraja. My favourite is from a Tamil text, *Unmai Vilakkam*: 'Creation arises from the sound of the drum [damaru]; protection proceeds from the [upraised] hand of hope; from the fire proceeds destruction; the foot held aloft gives release.' The dance is interpreted in terms of five activities, viz., creation, preservation, destruction, giving an appearance of illusion, and salvation or grace (*sristhi, sthiti, samhara, tirobhava,* and *anugraha*). It is also interpreted in terms of Yoga. The image is said to embody the inner processes by which the coiled kundalini or serpent-power is realized or straightened.

Nataraja's damaru, particularly, is a fascinating symbol. A small double-sided drum played with one hand, it is believed to be the source of the sound which creates—and recreates—the universe. It is also the source of the cosmic rhythm which influences the movement of energy in the universe. Shiva is said to have played the damaru twice; the first time nine sounds emerged while the second time five emerged, making a total of fourteen. Each one of these sounds was developed into a sutra upon which Sanskrit grammar is based, leading to the whole magnificent edifice of Sanskrit language and literature.

The image of the Nataraja reached its perfection under the Chola dynasty in south India between the AD 11th and 14th centuries. The Chola kings were the ones who built the great Shiva temples which are marvels of architecture, engineering, aesthetics, and sculpture. These include the great Brihadeshwara temple in Thanjavur, the beautiful temple at Tiruvannamalai, and the famous Nataraja temple at Chidambaram.

Chidambaram is where the Bharatanatyam dance originated and its 1000 postures are engraved in the temple complex. The story goes that two great Shiva devotees—Patanjali, author of the Yoga Sutra who is depicted as half man and half serpent; and Vyaghrapada, who was granted huge feet like those of a tiger so that he could more effectively gather flowers to offer Shiva—together prayed to Shiva saying that they missed his original dance in Kailasha, so would he kindly come and dance again in the 1000-pillared hall in Chidambaram, which is covered entirely with solid gold. Shiva agreed to their request and performed the dance. There is a beautiful Bharatanatyam dance connected with this legend called Natanam Adinar.

***

Shiva is often described only as the destroyer but this is inaccurate. As we have seen, Nataraja's Tandava involves both destruction and regeneration. He only destroys so that a new creation can become possible. Unlike the Semitic religions which postulate a sharp dichotomy between good and evil, creation and destruction, Hindu philosophy presents the tremendous concept of a deity in whom all paradoxes are accommodated and resolved, presenting an integrated vision of existence.

In Shiva worship, too, there are two polarities. The Nirguna Shiva is worshipped in the form of a Shivalinga, representing the creative power but in a static state. The other form is the Nataraja, the kinetic state, which represents the cycle of dissolution and regeneration. These are the two most widespread representations, but there are several others in sculpture and painting, both classical and folk. He is also a popular figure in calendar art and, in recent years, even psychedelic art. In his different forms Shiva combines apparent polarities which can appeal to people of various psychological profiles.

While Shiva is worshipped in thousands of shrines in South Asia and other parts of the world, there are twelve special shrines in India known as the Jyotirlingas which are considered particularly auspicious. They are spread across the country and traditionally are mentioned in the following sequence:

Somnath in Saurashtra (Gujarat)
Mallikarjuni in Srisailam (Andhra Pradesh)
Mahakaleshwar in Ujjain (Madhya Pradesh)

Omkareshwar in Amaleswara (Madhya Pradesh)
Vaidyanath in Parali (Maharashtra)
Nageswar in Darukavanam (Gujarat)
Kedareswar in Kedarnath (Uttarakhand)
Tryambakeswar in Nasik (Maharashtra)
Rameshwar in Setubandanam (Tamil Nadu)
Bhimashankar in Dakini (Maharashtra)
Visweswar in Varanasi (Uttar Pradesh)
Ghrishneswar in Devasrovar (Maharashtra)

These shrines are open to people of all castes, creeds, and colour because Shiva is the Universal Lord and these distinctions are meaningless before him.

While these are the major shrines, the worship of Shiva is widespread and ubiquitous throughout India. In thousands of villages there will be Shivalingas kept under trees and worshipped regularly. In Hinduism, each deity has its special form of worship, many of which involve elaborate rituals, clothing and jewellery, which can be quite expensive. The worship of Shiva, however, is very simple, which is why it is so widely prevalent. It simply involves pouring water on the Shivalinga while reciting a simple mantra, *Aum Namah Shivaya* (Aum, I bow to Shiva). Of course, in large Shiva temples more elaborate poojas are arranged, especially on auspicious days, the main celebration being Mahashivratri, which falls according to the Hindu calendar sometime in March. On that day, millions gather around India and abroad to worship Shiva in the evening after a day of fasting and prayer.

Interestingly, it is at the two ends of India that Shiva

worship reached its acme. In Kashmir, with its long and rich cultural history, a special branch of Indian philosophy known as the Trika Darshan or Kashmir Shaivism developed over the centuries. This school has its own sacred texts—the *Nigamas* and *Shiva Sutras*—and produced a whole series of outstanding philosophers, the greatest of whom was Acharya Abhinavagupta (AD 950-975). His massive contribution equals that of Adi Shankaracharya, but he was less well known because Kashmir Shaivism was confined largely to the Valley, whereas Shankaracharya travelled the length and breadth of the country. Just as remarkable, and at the other end of the subcontinent, is Tamil Nadu's Shaiva Siddhanta philosophy, which grew over the centuries to become one of the most powerful of all schools of Hinduism, receiving, as it did, the support of a series of dynasties.

Among the devotees of Shiva, the sixty-three Nayanars stand out for their devotion as well as their literary abilities. These Tamil poet-saints who lived between the AD 3rd and 8th centuries cover the entire spectrum of society, from powerful kings and prosperous merchants to oppressed Dalits. Their lives are related in a book called *Periya Puranam* by Chekkizhar. The remarkable life stories of the Nayanars all end with Shiva and Parvati, seated on their bull Nandi, appearing before the devotees.

***

Shiva is by no means confined to India. His worship was part of the culture of several South and Southeast Asian nations. In the magnificent temple complex at Angkor Wat there is an elaborate carving of Nataraja dancing above Brahma, Vishnu, Ganesha, and other celestial beings. On the outer wall of the great Prambanan Buddhist temple in Indonesia is a figure of the dancing Shiva, and in Yogyakarta, Java there is a group of three well preserved temples to Shiva, Vishnu, and Brahma. Nataraja also appears in Danang, Vietnam, and in several Central Asian countries. Thailand has its own beautiful Nataraja, as has Sri Lanka. Suffice to say that the powerful and unique image of Shiva Nataraja has found its way into one quarter of the globe. This a tribute to the remarkable power of this image of the kinetic Divine.

A number of missions propagate Shaivism around the world today. One of the most interesting that I have come across is the Shaiva Siddhanta Church on the island of Kauai in Hawaii, USA. This was founded by Gurudev Shivaya Subramuniya Swamy, a disciple of the great Shaiva guru of Sri Lanka, Sadguru Yogaswamy, in 1952. Gurudev has now passed away but the Himalayan Academy that he founded continues its activities, including a massive publishing programme. The Academy is set in lovely surroundings with a stream and a waterfall. It also has many rudraksha trees, the fruit of which when dried gives us rudraksha beads which are integral to Shiva worship. The swamis are all Americans and they work tirelessly to bring out a series of comprehensive books on Shaivism, the most important of which is *Dancing with Siva*, as well as a quarterly journal called *Hinduism Today*, which has a worldwide circulation.

***

Through the centuries, Shiva has inspired remarkable literature by devotees, scholars, thinkers, and philosophers, not only in India but around the world. The Nataraja in particular has become the image par excellence of Hinduism accepted, interestingly enough, also by many scientific organizations. The Nataraja image stands in famous locations such as the European Organization for Nuclear Research (CERN) laboratory for particle physics on the Franco-Swiss border, and the World Health Organisation in Geneva. Nataraja transcends any particular religion because Shiva himself accepts all without any discrimination. He is, after all, Vishwanatha, Lord of the world.

Here is a translation of a hymn to Mahadeva that I composed in Dogri some years ago:

Listen, oh listen to me, Shiva, great Lord,
I bow before You,
Grant me a vision of Your form today.
Darkness threatens to engulf me,
Light the candle of faith in my heart, Lord,
And grant me a vision of Your form today.

My frail bark is tossed ruthlessly about
On the turbulent ocean of relative existence,
Lead it safely to the other shore, Lord,
And grant me a vision of Your form today.
The eternal longing for Your blissful embrace
Throbs deep in my heart,
Fulfil this desire, Lord,
And grant me a vision of Your form today.

THE MESSAGE OF THE BHAGAVAD GITA

When we look at Indian civilization, particularly the great Hindu tradition, we have the Vedas stretching back into the very dawn of history, the great inspired utterances of rishis in thousands upon thousands of beautiful mantras. We have the Upanishads, the Vedanta, representing the culmination of the Vedas both philosophically and chronologically. We have the Brahma-Sutras, which give us an intellectual guide and key to the understanding of the Vedas. We have the Puranas, we have the epics, the *Ramayana*, and the *Mahabharata*. I earlier compared the great Himalayan range to the Vedas, and of the Upanishads as the mountain peaks. Now I will change the metaphor, and talk of the starry sky at night. Nothing is more magnificent and beautiful than looking up at the sky on a moonless night, when you see thousands upon thousands of celestial bodies all glowing with inner power and light. But among these you will notice that there is one star that shines brighter than the others. It may not be bigger, it may not be closer, but it is the brightest star-what we know as the 'morning star' or as Venus. And as we look at this great galaxy of Hindu texts and scriptures, there is one star that shines brighter than the rest, and that is the Bhagavad Gita

The Gita occupies a unique place, even though it is *smriti*—'what is remembered'—whereas the Vedas and the Upanishads are shruti—'what is said'—and the latter are considered superior in their authenticity and chronology. But the Gita has a very special position. Adi Shankaracharya, in one of his memorable shlokas, says that anyone who has tasted even a drop of amrita, the sacred elixir, or who has understood even a little of the Bhagavad Gita, need not have any fear of death. The Gita has been commented upon by all the great philosophers—by Shankara and Madhva, by Ramanuja and Vallabhacharya, by Gyaneshvara, and, in our own century, by Bal Gangadhar Tilak and Sri Aurobindo, by Mahatma Gandhi and Vinoba Bhave. In my view, after Shankaracharya's commentary, Sri Aurobindo's *Essays on the Gita* is the most luminous and magnificent of commentaries. Many leaders of our freedom movement were influenced by the Gita.

What is the reason for this extraordinary popularity of the Gita and its relevance to modern times. As I see it, there are four main reasons why the Gita is so tremendously significant and relevant in this age, and why it is the best known of the Hindu scriptures, and along with the Bible and the Quran, one of the three most influential religious texts in the history of mankind. The first reason is that the Gita was born in a situation of conflict—in the very midst of the great Kurukshetra war of the *Mahabharata*. Both the armies were drawn up, the flight of missiles had begun, the conch shells were sounded, the clamour of war was tumultuous and the hearts of the participants were torn by the conflict. It is then that the Gita teaching came to us, it is then that Krishna called upon Arjuna to arise to get ready for battle. The Gita is a scripture of conflict, whereas the Upanishads are set in a very calm and peaceful atmosphere.

Let us remember that Kurukshetra is not only a physical space, a plain in present-day Haryana. This outer Kurukshetra is still there, of course, but the inner Kurukshetra is within each one of us. It is within our psyche that the *asuri*, or demonic, and *daivi*, or divine, powers are drawn up in array against each other, and it is within the heart of our consciousness that this battle has constantly to be fought. Today, with the world poised on the brink of a mighty conflagration, it is a Kurukshetra situation for all humanity, and the Gita, a *sangharsha shastra* (scripture of conflict), is what the world needs—a stirring call to arms, not for personal aggrandizement, not even for national glory, but for the deeper, more difficult task of becoming an instrument of the divine will, a warrior for the divine cause, a fighter for the divine consciousness; for 'goodness'. That is the battle to which Krishna calls us, and that is why man today, torn as he is in a situation of conflict, responds to the message of the Gita.

The second reason for the importance and relevance of the Gita lies in the divine personality of the teacher. Every scripture has its guru, its *acharya*. The *Mundaka Upanishad* has Angiras, the *Brihadaranyaka Upanisad* has Yajnavalkya, and other seers and rishis are there, too. But in the Bhagavad

Gita it is the divine Lord Himself, disguised in a human form, who is talking to us. Krishna can be looked upon in many different ways. In one view, he is the personification of the Brahman, the Great Power which, shining, causes everything else to shine, which illuminates everything that exists—*tam eva bhantam anubhati sarvam, tasya bhasa sarvam idam vibhati* (Everything shines only after that shining light, His shining illumines all this world). In the eleventh chapter of the Gita, He appears in his great *virataswarupa* in which everything that exists is to be found, and by whose glory Arjuna is dazzled, as if a thousand suns had risen together upon the horizon.

And yet this very Krishna comes before us in the Gita as a charioteer, as a guide, as one holding the reins of the chariot. We have god Himself descended in the form of the divine charioteer, and that is why when Krishna speaks, he does so with absolute and overriding authority, not simply from the human standpoint but from the divine. That is why the Gita is so significant, because it personalizes the *Parabrahman* (the highest god-consciousness of the Upanishads). The Upanishads say: *Sarvam khalv idam brahma* (all this is Brahman); the Gita says: *Vasudevah sarvam iti* (all this is *Vasudevah*, the supreme). So, in the Gita the figure of Krishna personifies that divine splendour and power which is described so beautifully in the Upanishads, and that is why it has a unique impact upon our minds and hearts.

The third reason for the Gita's special importance lies in the relationship between the guru and the shishya. In the Hindu tradition this is a very intimate relationship. In the Upanishads the guru uses the term *saumaya* for disciple, meaning 'dearly beloved'; he looks upon the disciples as even more close to him than his own sons, because whereas the father only gives physical life the guru makes real spiritual birth possible. But in the Bhagavad Gita there is a closeness between Arjuna and Krishna which is not, as far as I am aware, to be found in any other scripture. One of the most moving verses of the Bhagavad Gita is when Arjuna, after he sees the *virataswarupa*, says to Krishna: 'I bow to you, I prostrate myself before you, and I demand grace from you. Like a father to his son, like a friend to his dear friend, like a lover to his beloved, do thou bear with me? Where else in the scriptures of the world would you get this composite relationship; the love between a father and a son, between a friend and a dear friend, between a lover and the beloved, all combined in the relationship between Krishna and Arjuna. That is what makes it so significant. It is a relationship of trust, faith, and devotion. Krishna is urging his friend, not threatening him. At the end of his entire teachings, Krishna says to Arjuna: *yathe 'cchasi tatha kuru* (do as you please). He says, in effect: 'I am not forcing you, I am not threatening you, I am not cajoling you. You asked me a question and I have shown you the path. It is now your decision, you have to do what you like.'

It is this aspect of the Gita which makes the teaching so significant and attractive, especially for the younger generations, because the youth, not only in India but throughout the world, is not prepared to be bullied or badgered by the older generation, or to accept their claim to superior wisdom or knowledge or morality. However, if we guide them with love, if we are friends with them, then perhaps we can influence them more effectively.

A fourth reason for the importance of the Gita is its universal applicability. The Gita as a doctrine does not confine itself to any particular creed. In the tenth chapter, Krishna is very clear: 'In whichever way people approach me, as long as they do it with faith, I make that resolve firm.' What an amazing assertion this is! Hinduism does not generally wish to make converts, because it is aware that the divine Atman is residing in all beings. Who is it ultimately that it will convert? The universal applicability of the Gita and its wide, all-embracing doctrine is extremely important. It is not a narrow creed. Again and again Krishna in the Gita says that, 'whatever faith one may have, ultimately that worship will come to him.' That is why the Gita has such a great appeal not only to Hindus but to genuine spiritual seekers whatever religion they may belong to.

Let us turn now to the content of the Gita. It is multifaceted and many-dimensional; a single shloka can be taken up and developed for days as has been done by many commentators. But, briefly, I will place before you four major aspects of the teachings of the Gita which I consider to be particularly significant. The first is the theory of correct action. I have said that the Gita is a *sangharsha sastra* and the problem in war is: what is to be done? Indeed, at any given point of time in our lives, whether we are students or in business or in politics or in any other field of life, the question always is: what is to be done, what is our *kartavyam karma*?

This is the most difficult of all questions. The Gita itself realizes this, and at one point Krishna says: *Gahana karmano gatih* (Thick and tangled is the way of action). The theory of correct action in the Gita revolves around a single concept; that action should not be purely for selfish purposes, although the self is obviously involved; it should not be simply a necessary evil, because we have to act. Action must be a positive, joyous, affirmative action, it must be an offering to the divine. This is the important point. It does not really matter what it is we are doing, what is important is the psychological and spiritual input into that action. In the eighteenth chapter there is a very important shloka which says that by worshipping through one's action, the divinity that pervades the entire cosmos moves man toward perfection.

So, there you have the answer. It has to be an action which is skilful, which is efficient, but which tries to avoid obsession, because obsessive action can easily become self-negating. If the action is detached, there is an inner freedom and inner dedication and you do not become obsessed. I have met so many people in my life, particularly in politics, people of great gifts; but they become so obsessed with their action and the result of the actions that ultimately they destroy themselves as human beings. We must have involvement without attachment and commitment without obsession. It is a very difficult path. Involvement we need, but without attachment. If you do not get involved, then you are evading your responsibility; but if you get attached, you are distorting your consciousness. Similarly, commitment without obsession, that is the special type of action that the Gita gives us.

There is a story about the building of the great Brihadisvara temple a thousand years ago by Rajaraja Chola in Thanjavur, probably the most beautiful temple in India. The king one day decided to go and inspect the work; so, he drove to the temple site, got out of his chariot and walked towards where this temple was being built. He came across a man who was cutting stones, and he asked him: 'What are you doing?' The man said: 'Sir, I am cutting stones.' He went a little further, and there was another man who was doing the same thing. He said: 'What are you doing?' The man answered: 'Sir, I am earning a living. He went further and came to a third person who was doing exactly the same thing. He asked: 'What are you doing?' He said: 'Sir, I am building a great temple.' We see the difference in attitude. They were doing exactly the same thing, they were getting exactly the same wages. But the first man was mechanically performing a task, he had no greater consciousness. The second one had a slightly broader vision, he had the problem of his family and was earning for them. The third one was earning for his family certainly, but he had the broad vision that he was building a great temple to Lord Shiva. That illustrates the theory of correct action. Whatever you may be doing, it does not really matter as long as you are doing it with inner dedication and devotion, and as long as you are using action itself as a powerful means of spiritual development. This is the first major teaching of the Gita, the theory of correct action.

Second, there is the theory of an integrated yoga that the Gita places before us. The four yogas, the four paths to divine union—gyana yoga, the way of wisdom, of intellectual discrimination; bhakti yoga, the way of emotional outpouring towards a personalized image of the divine; karma yoga, the way of dedicated action; and raja yoga, the way of psychic discipline, of *pranayama*, the discipline of breathing control, and the development of the kundalini shakti (serpent power) within us. These are the four main types of yogas that we have in our tradition, and for each there are scriptures which deal with various aspects. Thus, for the gyana yoga we have the Upanishads; for the karma yoga we have the *Karma-kanda*; for the bhakti yoga we have the *Srimad Bhagavatam*, the *Shiva Purana* and other Puranas; and for the raja yoga we have Patanjali's Yoga Sutra and other texts. But the Gita is unique in that, in the short compass of 700 shlokas, it integrates these four yogas into a single, unified path.

The Gita points out that it is no longer enough for us to follow only one of these paths. In the old days, if you were a *gyani* you could go off into the mountains in Kashmir and sit there for the rest of your life meditating, but that is not good enough for the Kali-yuga, the age we live in. In the old days, if you were a *bhakta*, you could spend your entire life going around doing kirtan. If you were a *raja yogi*, you could sit in your own ashrama and develop your powers. If you were a *karma yogi*, you could wander around doing good deeds. But it is not enough now for us to be one of these; we have to be all four. Every individual has to develop his mind, his heart, his physical capacity and his inner spiritual power, and that is the important message of the Gita. It brings us to what Sri Aurobindo calls *purnayoga*, an integrated yoga.

Third, there is in the Gita a repeated reassurance of divine intervention. You are familiar with the popular shloka where Krishna says that from age to age, whenever unrighteousness flourishes and *dharma* is about to disappear, he will assume human form for the destruction of the evil-doers and re-establishment of the *dharma*. This is an assurance given to all humanity, and, if we read the Gita with an open mind and have faith in it and Krishna, we must accept this assurance at its face value. It is not simply a bit of hyperbole in which he was indulging. I think today the time has come when we have got to ask Krishna why he is not fulfilling the assurance that he gave us. Surely, if we need the divine, the divine also in some way needs us. Krishna had the Sudarshana Chakra (thousand-spoked discus); he could have used it and finished the terrible Kurukshetra war himself. Why did he not do it? He also needed Arjuna, may be the latter's role and significance was *nimitta-matram*—just to a minuscule degree—but Krishna needed the *nimitta*, the minuscule; otherwise, he could not have won the war of *Mahabharata*, at least not in the way it was won. Perhaps, one could ask—if we need the divine, does the divine not need us? Does the supramental power, does the greater consciousness that is seeking to descend or to emerge, not need active co-operation from us? I think it does, and I assert that, as Sri Aurobindo puts it, without an aspiration from below there will not be an answering call from above. And that is why it is so important that we shun the attitudes of dejection, despair, and negativism that one finds so often in India; people constantly bemoaning and bewailing their lot and saying that the country is going to the dogs and that everything is breaking down. It is no use moaning and groaning like that, it will get us nowhere. We have to arise and be ready to fight the battle of existence. If our lives end before it is completed, so what? We have had thousands of lives before, and we will have thousands more. The Atman, as the Gita says, cannot be burnt, cannot be cut, cannot be drowned, cannot be cleaved. But we must have faith; faith in our own inner capacity and in the assurance of Krishna.

I have spoken of the theory of correct action, of the integration of the four yogas, the four paths to spiritual development, of the repeated assurance of divine intervention. Finally, we come to the Gita's gospel of total surrender to the divine. Ultimately, at the end of the entire discourse, after Krishna has said: *yathe 'cchhasi tatha kuru*, once again he speaks; without a question this time, he speaks on his own. All the rest of his speeches were in response to questions from Arjuna, but the last statement of Sri Krishna is suo moto. And he says: *Sarvadharman parityajya mam ekam sharanam vraja, aham tva sarvapapebhyo mokshaishyami ma suchah*—

What is *dharma*? (*Dharma* comes from the root dhri, 'that which supports'.) In the final analysis, what is it that supports human consciousness? It is not wealth, it is not position, it is not political power, howsoever important these may appear to us. Ultimately, it is the divine consciousness that supports us, that supports our very existence. Therefore, Krishna urges us to give up all other supports and come alone to him. Krishna speaking as the divine himself says, *Sarvadharman parityaja*...:

'Give up all other *dharmas* and seek refuge in me; I will free you from all sin. Do not fear.' How much love there is in those two words: 'Do not fear'. This is similar to a parent reassuring a child who has to enter a dark room and the parent says: 'Do not be afraid, I am here; go ahead.' These words—*ma suchah*—in a way sum up the entire message of the Gita. Let us not be afraid, and let us give up all lesser supports so that ultimately we get the one true support, the only thing that can support the growth and development of the higher consciousness, the grace of the divine.

Krishna's flute is still playing in Vrindavana. We may not be able to hear it because our ears are so full of the clamour and noise of daily living, and the conflicts and the tensions around us, but it is still playing. And Krishna is still there as the charioteer riding with us in our own higher consciousness. We do not have to go back to Kurukshetra, we do not have to go back to Arjuna. Krishna is with us always, provided we have ears to listen, provided we have eyes to see, provided we do not get totally blinded and deafened by the outer material conflicts which surround us. The outer is also important, but ultimately it is he whose inner consciousness is firmly centred in the divine, he alone, who will be able to meet the conflicts that lie ahead.

Conflicts will always be there. There is no easy path to greatness or to spiritual realization, either individual or collective. We must always remember the Vedic exhortation: *Charaiveti, charaiveti* (Move on, move on). Imagine human consciousness as a great current that is flowing down through the dark channels of time. If we do not swim upwards against the stream, we will be carried down to the rapids and the waterfalls below. There can be no standing still for man. Man is a transitional being, half way between the animal and the divine. Man's destiny is to move onwards to the next stage of evolution, for then only can our divine nature be fully developed. But, in order to move upwards, we have to struggle. If we have faith and reverence, then, with the sound of the divine flute echoing in our ears and the voice of the divine charioteer resounding in our hearts, we can move resolutely onwards towards the divine destiny that awaits us. That, in essence, is the message of the Gita.

THE MISSION OF SWAMI VIVEKANANDA

Why is it that India survives through the centuries, through the ages, when many other great civilisations that have arisen, in the long and tortuous course of human history, have fallen by the wayside? There have been other great civilisations; there was Greece, and Rome, there was Babylon, there were the great civilisations of Central and South America. But today those civilisations live on only in their ruins, or in the four walls of museums or in the minds of scholars. But India, despite a million shocks and a million tribulations, despite upheavals that would have shattered many a lesser civilisation, continues to retain its living and glorious link with the very dawn of history. What is the reason for this? It seems to me, looking back on the long vista of Indian history, that the main reason is that whenever the light in this country has threatened to go out, whenever dark clouds of ignorance or disaster have gathered menacingly over India, there have always been born great men and women who have rekindled the light and the hope of this nation. This is true not only in the dark depths of that Ashtami when Krishna was born amidst the terror and the horror of Kamsa's reign; but also, throughout the long vista, a Buddha was born, a Shankara was born, and great saints and devotees were born in different parts of the country. And, at the very moment when it appeared that, once and for all, India is going to be extinguished, these people came and reilluminated our minds. They rekindled that Eternal Faith that has been burning in India ever since the dawn of our history. This is the main reason why India has survived while all other great, ancient civilisations of the world have fallen by the wayside.

One such moment in India's history was in the middle of the 19th century. After 1857, the last spark of resistance to alien rule had been stamped out. And India lay crushed and broken at the feet of her foreign conquerors. At that time, it was a subjugation, not merely political or military, but even more so, spiritual and intellectual. India had begun not only to lose faith in herself, but to decry her own past and her own tradition. There was an intellectual and spiritual void in this country. And it appeared that after surviving for so many thousands of years India was at last ready to fall and to pass on into the history of ruined civilisations.

But what happened again in the 19th century? As you are aware, at that very moment, when the night was the darkest, at that very moment when there seemed to be no hope whatsoever for a revival, a resurgence, in fact, began. And that resurgence, as you are aware, began first in Bengal, which was the province which the British first conquered, the province which felt the impact of British rule earlier than the rest of India. It is a magnificent story. the story of the Indian Renaissance, beginning with Baja Ram Mohan Roy, the founding of the Brahmo Samaj; later the Adi Brahmo Samaj and the Brahmo Samaj of India, led by Maharshi Devendranath Tagore and Keshab Chandra Sen; then the founding of the Prarthana Samaj in Maharashtra by Ranade and Bhandarkar; then the founding of the Arya Samaj in the Punjab by that human dynamo Dayanand Saraswati; and so on—a number of reform movements spread across the country. The Theosophical Society also did a great deal to bring about a resurgence in us as a people. But, all these, in a way, were peripheral to the mainstream of Hindu thought and Hindu tradition. A real revolution in this country required a revolution at the centre. A revolution merely in the periphery was not enough. And this revolution took place, revolving around one of the greatest men that the world has ever known, Sri Ramakrishna Paramahamsa.

It was an astounding phenomenon how Sri Ramakrishna, an untutored, unlettered person from a village, came to Calcutta and became a spiritual beacon for millions; how by the force of his unique *sadhana*, his unique *siddhi*, he was able to attract to his feet the greatest intellectuals and the greatest politicians of the day; and how Sri Ramakrishna at Dakshineswar became a flaming beacon of Light and Hope in the midst of the darkness that at that time pervaded India. It is a fascinating story, this of Sri Ramakrishna, and the point that I wish to make is that he represented a new Spiritual Resurgence in this country. And, among the many great and humble people that he attracted to his feet was one Narendranath Datta, who was later to become famous the world over as Swami Vivekananda.

Swamiji's life was a brief one. He lived for only thirty-nine years. And yet what magnificent achievements there were in this short period! His life was exciting and interesting—his early boyhood; his meeting with the Master, his discipleship; then after the passing away of Sri Ramakrishna, his wandering the length and breadth of India, mingling with princes and with paupers and getting an idea of the requirements and the needs of this nation; then his historic triumph in the West at the Parliament of Religions in Chicago, which by the sheer force of his personality he was able to dominate; and then further, his work in the US and in England; his triumphant return to India; his lectures from Kanyakumari to Kashmir, which inspired and revivified this nation; his founding and consecration of the Belur Math; and finally his passing away, his Maha Samadhi, in 1902, leaving behind him a glorious and unique chapter in the history of India.

Swami Vivekananda achieved in a very short span of time a virtual restatement of Hinduism to meet the requirements of the age. As mentioned earlier, this restating of eternal truths has been the key to the continuance and the subsistence of India. The truths remain the same because they are Eternal. If there is a spiritual truth, it cannot change from age to age or from time to time. But what can change and what does change is the statement of that truth, the presentation of that truth, to meet the requirements of different eras. And Swami Vivekananda, almost single-handed, was able to achieve a complete re-statement of Hinduism to meet the requirements at the end of the 19th century. And his message was to a very large extent responsible for bringing about a resurgence which took various shapes, including the great political movement. Today his message is needed more than ever before, because today, although we have achieved political freedom, we are nevertheless again facing an intellectual and spiritual void. The old is breaking, and passing away never to return, the new is yet to be born, and we find ourselves precariously poised between these two, groping for a new integration, for a new vision, for a new way of integrating the problems that face us. At a time like this, I think the message of Swami Vivekananda can be extremely valuable, extremely useful, to us. And, therefore, I will try and place before you, as I see them, some of the salient features of Swamiji's teachings.

Swamiji once wrote that his ideal can be put into a few words. And that is to preach unto mankind their divinity and how to make it manifest in every moment of life. This was his basic message. There are many facets of his teachings. I think the first is the Unity of all Religions. Not merely tolerance of religions—I would like to make this point, because tolerance is essentially a negative attitude. Tolerance merely means the absence of opposition. That is not what he preached. His was a positive acceptance of the unity of all religions. He was preaching the old Rig Vedic dictum:

Ekam Sat Vipraha Bahudha Vadanti

(Truth is one, the wise call it by many names.)

Chamundeshwari Temple, Mysore, one of the 18 Shakti Peethas.
(Photo by Bikash Das; Wikimedia Commons.)

Brahma, Vishnu and Shiva—the Trinity—with their consorts, Saraswati, Lakshmi and Parvati, respectively. (Miniature from Guler, c. 1770.)

Samudramanthan—the churning of the Ocean of Milk by the devas and the asuras. (Miniature, Maharashtra region, early 19th century.)

Devi, or Durga, mounted on a lion, slays the demon Mahishasura.
(Kalighat painting from Bengal, 19th century.)

Sculpture of Nataraja and Harihara (the composite form of Vishnu and Shiva) in the 8th-century Bhairavakona rock cut cave temples, Andhra Pradesh. (Photo: Sara Welch; Wikimedia Commons.

Bhudevi, the Earth-goddess. (Tamil Nadu, 13th century, Los Angeles County Museum of Art.)

Nataraja statue outside CERN, the European Council for Nuclear Research, in Geneva. (Peacearth; Wikipedia.)

Opposite page: Vishnu's Vishvaroopa, the cosmic form revealed, among others, to Arjuna during the *Mahabharata* war. (Punjab Hills, Bilaspur, c. 1740.)

Sculptures in the Prambanan Shiva Temple complex, Java. (Photos by—left to right—Anandajoti Bhikku, courtesy Wikimedia Commons, and Giovanni Boccardi, courtesy UNESCO.)

Rama and his brothers studying in the gurukula of Sage Vashishtha.
(Miniature, Bikaner, early 18th century; National Museum, New Delhi.)

Krishna explaining dharma to Arjuna during the battle of Kurukshetra.
(Miniature, c. 1800; Salar Jung Museum.)

Achyutam form of Krishna at Sri Sri Priyakant-ju Temple, Vrindavan.
(Photo: Kridha20; Wikimedia Commons.)

A woman praying in the Madurai Meenaskshi Temple.
(Photo: Claude Renault; Wikimedia Commons.)

Opposite page, top: The ice Shivalinga in the Amarnath Cave.
(Photo by Gangadhar Tambe; Wikimedia Commons.)

Opposite page, bottom: Pilgrims on the way to Kedarnath. (Photo by Phani2; Wikimedia Commons.)

Morning aarti on the banks of the Ganga in Varanasi.
(Photo: jeminichronicles; Wikimedia Commons.)

Women pray to Surya, the sun god, on Chhath Puja. (Photo: Bdeb1; Wikimedia Commons.)

A sadhu bathing in Allahabad, or Prayagraj, during the Maha Kumbh. (Photo: Vitthal Jondhale; Wikimedia Commons.)

A devotee in Varanasi. (Photo: Juan Antonio Segal; Wikimedia Commons.)

Or the *Mundaka Upanishad*:

> *Yathan Nadyah Syandamaanaah Samudre Astam gacchanti Naamaroope Vihaaya*
> *Tathaa Vidwaan Namaroopaad Vimuktah Paraat Param Purushamupaiti Divyam*
>
> (As streams arising from different parts of the country find their way ultimately to the same ocean, so do the various religions that have arisen here and throughout the world lead ultimately to the same spiritual goal.)

This was something that Swamiji taught, not merely as an intellectual exercise, but, born out of deep conviction and deep realization, because you will recall that Sri Ramakrishna in the course of his unique *sadhana* had actually experienced the unity of various religions. He had lived for several days as a Muslim and had had a vision of a divine personage who, he thought, was the Prophet of Islam. He had lived as a Christian and had a vision of the Christ of Christianity. And so, the unity of religions preached by Sri Ramakrishna and Swami Vivekananda was not merely something that is politically advantageous just because we happen to have a lot of non-Hindus in this country (that is the way in which many people preach secularism today). That was not their secularism. It was in a glowing and dynamic unity of religions. And I think that this is something, which today we must once again realise. All too often, we take what we call a secular stance because we feel that it is politically necessary to do so because India is inhabited, apart from the Hindus, by many crores of

Muslims, Christians, Buddhists, Sikhs, Jains, Parsis, and so on. I do not think that is the correct attitude. There may be a narrow political advantage, but the real attitude is to accept the unity of the goal of all religions and this is to my mind one of the most important teachings of Swami Vivekananda.

The second aspect is the divinity of man. Now the Divinity of god is not a very novel concept, because, after all, if there is a god, he is bound to be divine. There is nothing very special about it. But what do the Vedas and the Upanishads preach us? They preach the divinity of man. The Upanishads have a wonderful term for the human race: *Amruthasya Puthra* (Children of Immortality). What an extraordinarily bold and powerful concept this is! That every human being born on this planet, whether he is rich or poor, whether he is a Hindu or a Muslim or belongs to any other faith, whether he is born in India or in the Antarctic or any other part of the world, he is a 'Child of Immortality!' immortality is his birthright. This is something which Swamiji always used to stress. And he always used to say that it is not merely the rich, or people belonging to a community or caste that must be considered divine, but it is the entire mankind. And this concept of the divinity of man, therefore, cuts across all creeds, cuts across all nationalities, and embraces within its ambit the entire human race.

Closely flowing from this concept of the divinity of mankind is the dignity of the individual. Swamiji had a deep agony at the suffering that was present at that time in India. And he often used to say that religion is not for empty bellies; that if you want a person to be religious, you must first of all feed him at least the minimum necessary, you must clothe him, you must house him. Then only can you expect him to really start thinking about the things of the Spirit. Here again Western commentators often make a serious mistake. They think that Hinduism teaches poverty and renunciation and, therefore, there is no impetus, there is no incentive to economic development. This is complete nonsense, if I may say so. The poverty that Hinduism teaches is a voluntary renunciation—is the poverty of a Buddha who gave everything up in order to become poor. It is not a hereditary poverty. It is not that everyone should be born poor and, therefore, everyone will get spiritual bliss. It all seems self-evident to us. But I have heard a number of Westerners, and even a number of Indians, say 'Look, Hinduism preaches poverty.' It is a voluntary poverty. And you cannot be voluntarily poor unless first of all you are rich. For a man who is born poor, for a beggar, there is no spiritual advantage in his poverty. Therefore, Swami Vivekananda always used to stress the dignity of the individual. And this dignity of the individual cuts across all the ridiculous taboos and superstitions that went by the name of Hinduism at that time and that still to some extent deface and disfigure the features of India. For example, the whole question of untouchability. If there is divinity in every man, by what reasoning, by what logic, by what intellectual gymnastics, is it possible for us to say that a certain person is untouchable and that by touching him or by allowing him into the temple you profane and you spoil the temple into which he enters? I think that there can be no greater aberration of the spirit of the Vedas and Upanishads than this. And Swamiji used to say that if your religion is such a weak and paltry thing that it gets broken by touching, let it break; the sooner this sort of kitchen religion breaks and shatters to the ground, the sooner will India regain her strength and her pristine glory. This is something which Swamiji constantly preached. Again, this ridiculous belief that existed at that time, of *Prayaschitta*! There was a time in India when people went abroad and carried the message of India to the four corners of Asia; and then there came a time when if anybody went to England, before he was received back into his community, he had to go through this *Prayaschitta*, in order to wash away the pollution that he was supposed to have gathered abroad. What greater contrast could there be between the bold, all-inclusive aspect of Hinduism and these narrow superstitions and dogmas that have defaced the name of Hinduism through the ages! So Swamiji thundered against these. He was the greatest critic of a great deal of what goes by the name of Hinduism; because anything that went against his concept of the dignity and divinity of the individual was anathema to him.

Following again from this is the whole concept of service to society. He did not merely believe in a personal salvation, up in the mountains of the Himalayas. But he felt that it is by service of the *Daridranarayana*, by the service of suffering humanity that one's personal *sadhana* can also develop. And that is why he founded the Ramakrishna Mission which until this very day is performing extremely valuable service not only in India but throughout the world. Now this is a very important problem also, because there are many of us who are often tempted to leave the bustle, the heat and the struggle of active involvement and to go away into the beautiful calm of the Himalayas and to sit there and meditate upon the Eternal. I happen to come from the Himalayas incidentally and therefore I know perhaps the tremendous attraction that the mountains have. Unless you have lived in the mountains, unless you have been born there and brought up there, it is difficult to appreciate the special quality, the special magnetism that the mountains have...And it is difficult, therefore, to appreciate the extent of the conflict that often arises between involvements and withdrawal. But Swamiji did a unique thing. He combined the intense activity of the West with the deep meditation of the East and he put before us a glowing synthesis of the two. He showed us that in order to achieve our own spiritual development it was not necessary to go out into the Himalayas; it was necessary rather to alleviate the suffering of the masses of India. And this concept, I think, is as valid today, if not more, as it was when he first expounded it.

Then again—and this is also an important facet of his teaching—his deep and glowing love for India. When he swam across the small stretch of ocean at Kanyakumari and sat on the rock at the feet of Mother India where three oceans mingle and he looked up at this great and magnificent country that has nurtured our race for thousands of years, he had a vision of an India that was reborn, spiritually, economically, politically, an India that was resurgent, an India in which the suffering and the misery of lakhs of people would be alleviated, an India in which everybody would be proud to call himself an Indian. That was the vision that he saw. And that was the vision that throughout his lectures in the length and breadth of this country he tried to give to the people of India.

Today, I think, that is required even more than before, because, although we have achieved political freedom, we often find petty loyalties rising to the fore; petty regionalism, linguistic differences, casteism, and political schisms combine to shatter the unity of India that has been won after such great struggle and such great sacrifices. People talk of the north and the south and the east and the west and they talk of their own smaller loyalties, but how many people are there who talk of this glowing vision of a united and dynamic India that Swami Vivekananda put before us?

I am not one of those who decry the importance of region or of language in our lives. Certainly, it is there; it has its place, but its place is not a predominant one. Its place must be subordinated to the greater good of this nation of ours. Today, there are signs again that the vision of Swami Vivekananda is beginning to fade; there are signs that the unity of this great nation from Kashmir to Kanyakumari and from Dwaraka to Kamarup is once again being threatened—this time not so much by an external enemy as by our own internal weaknesses, and our own internal schisms. I think the vision that Swami Vivekananda had of India requires to be reiterated again and again so that we can place before ourselves this ideal of a united India.

And his vision even transcended India, because he was no

mere narrow chauvinist. He felt that a free India had a duty not only to itself but also to the entire world community. All the great thinkers in India have felt that—Swami Vivekananda, Sri Aurobindo—with his concept of evolutionary spiritualism and the concept that India has a special role to play in the development of the human race, and Jawaharlal Nehru with his emancipated and wide internationalism. This is a tradition that has been going on in India, because once you accept the divinity of the human race, you are ultimately not able to stop merely at India, because surely those living in Pakistan also belong to the same human race, and those living in China also. So, despite our political differences, we have got to retain the concept of *Vasudhaiva Kutumbhakam,* the world as the single family, and we have got to press for it.

And, Swami Vivekananda thought that India has a special destiny in bringing about this world-consciousness.

And in order to achieve all this, what did Swamiji tell us to be? He told us to be strong—not the strength of the Asuras, not the strength of a Hitler or a Mao, but the *Daivic Shakti*—the strength of the spirit, the fearlessness, the *Abhbyata*. Even the Upanishads say: *Nayamatma Balahinena Labhyaha*: the Atman is not to be attained by the weak. You cannot achieve anything in this life, whether it is material, or whether it is spiritual, if you are weak. So Swamiji taught the doctrine of spiritual strength, the doctrine that physically, intellectually, and spiritually we have to be strong. We have got to be strong. Then only, can we throw off the shackles of foreign rule, and the even more powerful and the more insidious shackles of our own weaknesses, of our own fears, because after all there is nobody and no power that can enslave us if we are free within. This has been demonstrated again and again in the long course of Indian history. And, Swamiji in his words of glowing wisdom and power said that if there is anything that makes you weak, it cannot be true. And he wrote at one place: 'And here is the test of truth—anything that makes you weak, physically, intellectually, and spiritually reject as poison. There is no life in it; it cannot be true. Truth is strengthening.'

This is what he taught. And, this is particularly what our younger generation has got to learn. Swamiji used to say of the youth: 'We want young Indians with muscles of iron and nerves of steel.' And the young people in India can do no better than to derive inspiration from the glowing words that Swami Vivekananda preached to us. This to my mind then is the message of Swami Vivekananda. This is the vision of that dynamic India. Today, we have got to live up to that.

Are we capable of fulfilling the vision that Swamiji saw? It is not merely enough to write essays, deliver lectures, or to listen, unless we take a vow that we will try to realize the vision that Swamiji has laid before us. Today is as good a day as any for us to rededicate ourselves to the mission that Swami Vivekananda laid before us, the mission of building a new India. Certainly, there will be difficulties. It is not an easy path. It is narrow. It is beset with dangers. It is sharp as a razor's edge. But without difficulties, nothing is achieved. And, no nation can become great, no people can become great if they do not have within them the power and the wisdom to overcome all difficulties. And, therefore, here is the great saying from *Kathopanishad* that Swami Vivekananda used to preach, the doctrine of power and wisdom:

> *Uthishtata Jagrata Prapya Varan Nibodhata, Kahurasya Dhara Nishita Durathyaya Durgam Pathasthat Kacayovadanti*
>
> Arise, awake, and learn by approaching the excellent ones. The wise ones describe that path to be as inaccessible as a razor's edge, which when sharpened is difficult to tread on.

THE ONE AND THE MANY

The one remains, the many change and pass;
Heaven's light forever shines, Earth's shadows fly;
Life, like a dome of many coloured glass,
Stains the white radiance of Eternity.

These words are by the great English Poet P.B. Shelley and express well the basic insights of Hindu philosophy. I believe that the entire cosmos is illuminated by the light of Brahman—the Ultimate Truth—which pervades not only our solar system but the billions and billions of galaxies in the unending universe around us. This is the spiritual correlate of the Unified Field Theory that the scientists are looking for to explain the entire multiplicity of material manifestation.

I also believe that there is a spark of that Divine in each individual, which is what gives us the capacity to live, to think and to function through our five senses. Without this spark we would be unconscious and immobile, so the one Supreme Light expresses itself through the many human beings and, to a lesser extent, through millions of living creatures on this planet. For me, the relation between the One and the Many is an integral, not a polarized one; in fact, it is a symbolic relationship. Therefore, fanning this spark into the blazing fire of spiritual illumination must be the ultimate goal of our religious rites, practices, and philosophies.

There is further elaboration of this in several of our Upanishads, which are the supreme texts of Hinduism, some of them dating back to 2000 years before the birth of Christ. These are extraordinary dialogues between the guru and one or more disciples, rather like the Socratic dialogues so memorably recorded by Plato. The great scientist Erwin Schrodinger said, 'The Upanishads have been the solace of my life, they will be the solace of my death.'

There is a particularly striking verse in the *Isha Upanishad* which translates as:

He who sees himself in all beings, and all beings within himself;
He who sees the Divine in all beings
For him what delusion, what sorrow
For he has seen the Oneness.

The real challenge is to try and incorporate these great principles into our daily life. This can best be done by interiorization, meditation, and prayer, and also by offering whatever we do to our preferred image or concept of the Divine.

Another aspect of the One and the Many in the Upanishads is that, unlike in later texts such as the *Ramayana* and the *Mahabharata*, there is no gender discrimination. One verse in the Upanishads says clearly and categorically: 'The Brahman is neither male nor female nor neuter, whichever body it inhabits, it takes on that identity.' In another verse it is said, 'He is this man, he is that woman, he is this boy, he is that girl. He is also that old man tottering along with a stick. He is born with his face turned in all directions.'

Of course, when dealing with the One and the Many it is not possible to ignore the fact that the Many are constantly involved in wars and other modes of conflict. The question arises that if they are all in fact parts of the One, then why should they be permanently at loggerheads? There are two contrasting scenarios for the future of the human race. Arthur Koestler in his book *Janus: A Summing Up*, has the view that there is a paranoid streak in human beings due to an engineering defect in the cortex whereby the thinking and the feeling aspects are not adequately integrated. As a result, although we know what should be done, we are unable to do it and, conversely, when we know that something should not be done, we go ahead and do it. Therefore, says Koestler, 'Man is a species programmed for self-destruction.'

I would like to recall a limerick in this connection. It goes as follows:

God's plan made a hopeful beginning
But man spoilt his chances by sinning
We know that the story
Will end in God's glory
But at present the other side's winning.

The jury is still out as to which side will finally prevail. All I can say is that each one of us in the crucible of our individual consciousness should strive to support the positive forces around us and not succumb to the negative ones.

When we look around and see the calamity of climate change, due largely to our own stupidity and insensitivity in the way we have cruelly exploited nature, thereby polluting the natural environment–land, air, and sea–and in addition see many ongoing fratricidal conflicts, the conflict between Russia and Ukraine and Israel and Hamas being the most recent; it is difficult to brush aside Koestler's grim prognosis. As against this we have the evolutionary philosophers like Teilhard de Chardin in the West and Sri Aurobindo in the East who hold that Man in fact is a work in progress and is 'a race destined to evolve into the higher consciousness'. The problem with the more optimistic view is that the time frame is very prolonged, while the destructive aspects are proceeding apace. In our analysis, therefore, we have to factor in the present situation and not only deal with theoretical possibilities. If the Many are in turmoil, what does it say about the One?

Let me here dwell a moment on the Interfaith Movement, the key to which is in the Rigvedic Mantra: *Ekam Sat Vipraha Bahudha Vadanti*—The Truth is One; the Wise call it by many names. The movement began in 1893 with the first Parliament of World Religions held in Chicago. Subsequently, these Parliaments have been held around the world. The goal of the Interfaith Movement is to foster a better understanding between the great religions of the world, and in this too the Upanishads show us the way.

From the dawn of history, terrible wars have been fought in the name of a god that every religion claims is compassionate and merciful. This is a cruel irony, as more people have been tortured and killed in the name of religion than in any other name. The Interfaith Movement seeks to bring together representatives of all the world's religions in a harmonious setting for a positive dialogue. I have been involved in this Movement for half a century but, regretfully, it has not had the required impact.

If we look at the political situation in the world during the 20th and the current century, we will notice that there is a strong tendency towards multiple conflicts and One strong person ruling the Many. In the 20th century, Hitler, Mussolini, Stalin, Mao, Pol Pot, and others were examples of one man's lethal domination over the Many, resulting in the death of millions. In our own century we already have Putin, Xi Jinping, and Erdogan and others. These examples demonstrate that one person can dominate millions usually with disastrous consequences. What spiritual message do we learn from this? Does this mean that only if the One is benevolent that it is acceptable, but when the One is cruel and rapacious it is not?

It is said that every nation has its own Karma and has to be analysed as such. Sri Aurobindo wrote extensively and emotionally about Bharat Mata (Mother India) but towards the end of his life he had also realised that nationalism is not enough, it has to transcend into a global society. Towards the end of the last century, I was very upbeat about the emerging global society. Remarkable developments like the European Union took place before my very eyes. My wife and I started travelling in Europe from 1956 and I recall all the different currencies–the Deutch Mark, the Franc, the Lira, the Pound–and all the visas that were needed while travelling. But miraculously the separate currencies disappeared and were replaced by the Euro, the visa requirements disappeared and were replaced by the Schengen, and the European Union emerged despite a history of centuries of lethal conflict between Germany, France, and the United Kingdom.

Idealists like me had hoped that similar developments would take place in other regional formations such as the Association of Southeast Asian Nations (ASEAN), the South Asian Association for Regional Cooperation (SAARC), North America Free Trade Agreement (NAFTA), and so on. Unfortunately, in the 21st century there has been a massive backlash against globalisation. Donald Trump denounced the concept by name, while around the globe, including India, the divisive and oppressive variety of nationalism has proved itself to be much more resilient than had been expected. As a result, the concept of a global society—'The Parliament of Man, the Federation of the World', as the poet Tennyson put it, seems to have evaporated. I wonder if we have made a substantive study of this area. I mention this because although we have the ancient Hindu concept of *Vasudhaiva Kutumbakam*—the World is a Family—we seem in fact to be heading in the opposite direction.

The Hindu view, I repeat, is that the Brahman, the

Ultimate Reality, is all encompassing—it is the One, and the many religions are different paths to try and reach the Divine consciousness. Hinduism is perhaps the only religion in the world that accepts multiple paths to the Divine and does not insist on any single path. One Truth–Many Paths is the key to the Interfaith Movement, as well.

***

Hinduism and the Interfaith Movement

The Interfaith movement, which should really be better known around the world has, as I have noted above in this essay, developed essentially over the 20th century, after the Parliament of the World's Religions held in Chicago in 1893 where, for the first time, representatives of all the world's great religions gathered for a mutually fruitful dialogue. It was there that, by a stroke of destiny, Swami Vivekananda, who was not even an invitee to the Parliament, appeared and made such a tremendous impact, which reverberates down to the present day by articulating the universal principles embedded in the Upanishads.

Over more than a century, several major Interfaith organisations have emerged, including the Temple of Understanding of which I happen to be President. This has resulted in a continuous series of meetings, conferences, seminars, and spiritual summits, all directed towards fostering harmony, understanding, and a creative dialogue between the world's great religions. In India also we have set up centres of the Temple of Understanding in several major cities around the country.

Hinduism is peculiarly well suited for this dialogue because of certain unique features. It is the only religion which does not trace its origins to any particular divine manifestation, prophet or book, and is based upon the collective spiritual insights of a whole galaxy of spiritually realised individuals—rishis and seers—spread over many centuries. As a result, there is tremendous scope in Hinduism for creative reinterpretation from age to age, and for articulating the eternal truths of the Vedanta in a manner suited to the changing social milieu. Indeed, that is precisely what such great figures—Swami Vivekananda, Sri Ramana Maharshi, Sri Aurobindo, and others sought to do.

Even before any of the other world religions emerged, Hinduism represented essentially a pluralistic and multi-faceted quest for divine realisation. It contains a vast variety of methodologies. One can worship a formless god, the *Nirakar* Brahman, or a divine with form—*Sakar* Brahman. In the latter, again, there is a wide variety—one can be a Shaiva, a Vaishnava, a Shakta or a combination of these and other paths. The basic point is that Hinduism has never postulated a single path to the divine. In fact, it harmonises a vast variety of beliefs without any contradiction.

It is in this context that one must view the relationship of Hinduism to the Interfaith movement. This is a long and complex story, but essentially it involves a generous and receptive attitude towards other religious beliefs; provided, always, that they do not seek to impose their views by force. Hindu-Christian dialogue, for instance, has over several decades been extremely rewarding. Men like Father Bede Griffiths, who could well be described as a Christian-Hindu and whose work in south India was outstanding, and Professor Raimundo Panikkar, whose *Mantramanjari*, an anthology of the Vedas, is a joy to read, represent the high watermark of this dialogue. In addition, many Christian leaders in India have had an excellent record of service in the field of health and education for all.

It is tragic that the great universal ideals and values of the world's many great faiths should be sullied by acts of violence, vandalism, and abuse. It remains my hope that all faiths can not only co-exist, but come together to heal humanity, and make spiritual and material wellbeing possible for everyone, everywhere.

Meanwhile, I end this essay with a poem written by Sri Aurobindo, the great evolutionary philosopher, whose massive corpus of work includes such classics as *The Synthesis of Yoga*, *The Human Condition*, *Essays on the Gita,* and his magnum opus, *The Life Divine*. The poem, an inspiration for our times that draws upon enlightened Hinduism, is entitled 'WHO', which evidently refers to the 'One' whose manifold manifestations illuminate the 'Many':

In the blue of the sky, in the green of the forest,
Whose is the hand that has painted the glow?
When the winds were asleep in the womb of the ether,
Who was it roused them and bade them to blow?

He is lost in the heart, in the cavern of Nature,
He is found in the brain where He builds up the thought:
In the pattern and bloom of the flowers He is woven,
In the luminous net of the stars He is caught.

In the strength of a man, in the beauty of woman,
In the laugh of a boy, in the blush of a girl;
The hand that sent Jupiter spinning through heaven,
Spends all its cunning to fashion a curl.

These are His works and His veils and His shadows;
But where is He then? By what name is He known?
Is He Brahma or Vishnu? A man or a woman?
Bodied or bodiless? Twin or alone?

We have love for a boy who is dark and resplendent,
A woman is lord of us, naked and fierce.
We have seen Him a-muse on the snows of the mountains,
We have watched Him at work in the heart of the spheres.

We will tell the whole world of His ways and His cunning:
He has rapture of torture and passion and pain;
He delights in our sorrow and drives us to weeping,
Then lures with His joy and His beauty again.

All music is only the sound of His laughter,
All beauty the smile of His passionate bliss;
Our lives are His heart-beats, our rapture the bridal
Of Radha and Krishna, our love is their kiss.

He is strength that is loud in the blare of the trumpets,
And He rides in the car and He strikes in the spears;

He slays without stint and is full of compassion;
He wars for the world and its ultimate years.

In the sweep of the worlds, in the surge of the ages,
Ineffable, mighty, majestic and pure,
Beyond the last pinnacle seized by the thinker
He is throned in His seats that for ever endure.

The Master of man and his infinite Lover,
He is close to our hearts, had we vision to see;
We are blind with our pride and the pomp of our passions,
We are bound in our thoughts where we hold ourselves free

It is He in the sun who is ageless and deathless,
And into the midnight His shadow is thrown;
When darkness was blind and engulfed within darkness,
He was seated within it immense and alone.

THE LIGHT AT THE HEART OF INDIA

The public debate regarding Hinduism and its various definitions has been a topic of animated political controversy in India since the early 1990s. To me, there is only one defining idea of Hinduism that supersedes all others: Hinduism is unique in that it is not tied to any one text, one individual or one point in time, and this gives it a remarkable built-in pluralism. The key to the continued dynamism of Hinduism despite so many challenges and persecutions from outside, and damage from within, lies in its remarkable capacity for creative rearticulation by a whole succession of seers and social reformers; but also, above all, in its spirit of, and capacity for, accommodation.

The master principles upon which Hinduism is based are to be found essentially in the Upanishads. In these luminous dialogues, the great issues confronting humanity have been addressed in a manner that will be difficult to find anywhere else. The most basic concept is that of the all-pervasive Brahman: *Isavasyam idam sarvam yat kincha jagatyam jagat*—Whatever exists and wherever it exists is permeated by the same divine power. While many philosophies have postulated unbridgeable dichotomies between God and the world, matter and spirit, person and person, the Upanishadic view is that everything that exists is 'One'.

Here is a philosophy which cuts across barriers of hatred and fanaticism that have been built in the name of religion. At its highest, Hinduism is a universalist religion. It accepts the infinite possibilities of movements towards the divine, and does not seek to limit or confine us to any particular formulation. Each one of us has to seek our own path, and Hinduism welcomes and accepts the multiplicity of paths to the divine. Thus, the seers of the Upanishads, the great Christian mystics, the Muslim Sufis, the Sikh gurus, all finally speak of a luminescent awareness of the divine presence.

So, an exclusivist approach to Hinduism would constitute a grievous injustice to this great faith and philosophy. When we demand that India, or Bharat, should be declared a Hindu nation, that everyone should submit to a narrow, oppressive formulation of a great faith, we damage both Hinduism and India.

It is certainly true that Hinduism has provided the broad cultural and religious framework that has held India together despite its astonishing linguistic, ethnic and political diversity, and divisions. Hinduism is as essential for an understanding of Indian culture and civilisation as Islam is for the Arab world and Roman Catholicism for Latin America. But many other religions have also flourished in India for centuries, and there are today quite a few states and Union territories where

Hindus are not in a majority, especially if we respect the wish of many Adivasi communities to be recognised as followers of distinct, animistic faiths. The rich, pluralistic cultural and religious mosaic that is India needs to be carefully nurtured.

It is also important to remember that India has by no means a monopoly over Hinduism. All Indians are not Hindus and all Hindus are not Indians. There are millions of Hindus living around the world who, while certainly having special regard for India as their spiritual motherland, are yet loyal and patriotic citizens of their respective countries. To equate 'Hindu' with 'India', therefore, is to create an avoidable conceptual confusion. Hinduism is one of the great religions of the world, and to seek to confine it to present-day India or to give it an exclusivist and majoritarian interpretation is to do it a disservice.

While every nation and every community has the right, indeed the duty, to defend itself against attack and aggression, we must never take on the role of the aggressor. Anyone who lives by the great ideals of Hinduism should, by definition, adopt an attitude of amity towards other religious traditions. This is the secularism—the light—at the heart of India. And it is not, as some people maintain, alien to our land. India has been—despite some aberrations—and must always remain, secular in spirit and practice.

Communalism and Religion

Not only in India but throughout the world religion has through the ages played two distinct roles in society. On the one hand, it has had the effect of unifying large sections of people who would otherwise have remained fragmented and fractured into petty tribes and principalities, thus, bringing about a tremendous degree of cohesion among large groups of human beings within and across nations. But, on the other hand, religion has also led to sharp and severe divisions between person and person, group and group, nation and nation. The history of mankind is replete with wars and crusades due to religious fanaticism, and within countries there have been large-scale riots and civil wars based upon religious differences.

There is, of course, a third aspect of religion, in fact its real and crucial role, which lies in providing the philosophical background and psychological motivation for the individual spiritual quest. But this has an individual rather than a sociological impact.

In India we can see all these aspects of religion clearly at work through the long vistas of our history. While a resilient, accommodative Hinduism has been largely responsible for the continuing unity of India, it is also true that since the advent of Islam there have been many occasions upon which the followers of these two great religions have come into bitter and severe conflict. The partition of India itself, despite the firm disavowal of the two-nation theory by the majority of Indians regardless of religious affiliation, was based essentially upon the breaking away of large sections of Muslim-majority areas. To that extent, Pakistan was the measure of our failure to integrate into the body politic of India large sections of the Muslim population.

However, despite the trauma of Partition, accompanied as it was by the most horrifying communal riots in which lakhs of innocent men, women, and children perished, it is a tribute to the enlightenment of our leaders and the inherent good sense of our people that we adopted a Constitution based upon complete equality for all religions, and that we have in fact been able to create a functioning secular democracy. It is true that our secularism is by no means fully successful, and that communal riots and bigotry continue to throw their baneful shadow over our body politic. It is also true that our law enforcement authorities are often unable to give protection to the victims of communal fury, and that since the early 1990s, there has been a growth in majoritarian sentiment. And yet, I submit that it would be wrong for us to get caught up in a paroxysm of self-denigration and join in the chorus of the prophets of doom who claim that there has been no progress in India since Independence. The fact is that India is one of the few largely free multi-religious societies in the world, providing opportunities for religious liberty to one-sixth of the human race. For all the recent aberrations, this is what the Constitution and, for the most part, our judiciary and civil society continue to ensure.

Communalism, however, persists. In many ways, of course, it is inevitable that in a vast, multi-religious nation like ours, each religious community should seek to follow its own customs and rituals. This is by no means unhealthy; indeed, like a large multi-coloured tapestry, the different religious traditions of India add to the richness of our total national personality. The danger arises only when commitment to the particular community to which we happen to belong is distorted into narrow sectarianism that gives rise to suspicion and animosity against other religions and caste groupings. It is then that the broad stream of religion and philosophy gets broken up into narrow, constricted channels in which all sorts of distasteful and malodorous infections flourish.

It is those blinded by a narrow-minded fanaticism, led by the absurd conviction that they alone are the repositories of truth and wisdom, who are mainly responsible for the suspicion and mistreatment of people belonging to other communities. Fanaticism and ignorance go well together, and are invariably accompanied by an utter lack of spiritual experience. Indeed, it is an almost mathematical dictum that fanaticism varies in inverse proportion to the degree of spiritual realisation. At its deepest, religion is an uplifting, widening, maturing phenomenon. The mystics of all the world's great religions are bound to each other by that deepest of all links—spiritual experience. It is the integral concept of religion, therefore, that has to be reiterated and made part of our educational system and our national life if the virus of communalism is to be finally destroyed. Unless this is done no amount of mere legislation or administrative precautions will really solve one of free India's greatest challenges.

Three Approaches to Secularism

Secularism is fundamental to free India and is built into the very structure of the Constitution under which we live today as citizens of a democratic society. However, the mere fact of constitutional provisions is not enough to ensure that the concept is fully grasped, and it is necessary that we should constantly analyse and fully understand the crucial importance of secularism in our national life. This is particularly important where the post-Independence generations are concerned, because for them the freedom struggle, Partition, and Independence are essentially historical and distant rather than personal and immediate events.

There is the danger—already apparent—that they may take sovereign, free, and largely stable India for granted, without realizing that the foundations of freedom and democracy have constantly to be strengthened by each successive generation if the mighty structure of resurgent India is to keep growing and remain glorious. It is in this context that we should analyse the important concept of secularism.

To my mind there are those who accept secularism through three approaches current in India today, all revolving around differing conceptions of religion. The first approach is of those who look upon religion merely as an anachronism from the dark ages, as organized superstition or, at best, as an interesting sociological phenomenon which is one of the burdens that the past has hung around the neck of the present. In this view, the sooner all religions were consigned to the dustbin of history, the better for all concerned. But this school of thought is realistic enough to appreciate the fact that Indians are on the whole a deeply religious people, and it therefore feels that secularism is the only rational and feasible approach that can be adopted. Thus, while fully committed to the concept of secularism, the commitment of this school of thought is based upon a rejection of religious values; it can, therefore, be termed the 'anti-religious approach to secularism'.

At the other end of the spectrum is what might be termed the utilitarian approach to secularism. This school of thought holds that it would have been extremely desirable if all the inhabitants of India had belonged to the Hindu faith, because India could then openly become a Hindu State. However, people of this group realise the inescapable fact that many crores of people living in this country are non-Hindus and that there is no real possibility of this situation being changed. As a result, they reluctantly have to accept the necessity of India being a secular State. From this point of view, secularism is a necessary evil, which must be endured—at least till the time the impossible is somehow made possible.

According to the third approach, to which I personally subscribe, both these attitudes are unsatisfactory and fail to provide a dynamic and positive theory of secularism. In this view, the true sanction behind secularism is that all religions are in fact so many different approaches towards the same Divine Reality. Just as numerous streams flow from many directions to join the same ocean, as many paths ascend from different directions to the same summit, so do the various religions that have developed among mankind through the ages have as their goal the same divine communion. If a divine reality exists—as I firmly believe it does—it must ultimately be the same for all human beings. However deep and abrasive may be the differences that divide various religions on the sectarian and denominational level, at the level of true religious experience these must necessarily be resolved into an integral and transcendent unity.

I would submit that this view of religion alone can give us a correct approach towards the whole concept of secularism, and help us neutralize communalism. Because when we accept the basic unity of all religions, we simultaneously imbibe the true spirit of secularism—neither as a rejection of religious values, nor as a merely utilitarian instrument which must be accepted as a necessary evil, but as a positive and dynamic force which must remain one of the cardinal tenets of the remarkable Indian Republic.

PART THREE

Travels of a Pilgrim

(1950s and 1970s)

AMARNATH
(1953)

Amarnath, the Immortal Lord. The very word has always held a strange fascination for me. I had felt ashamed that I had never visited this famous place of pilgrimage so near my home, while thousands of people from the farthest corners of India made the pilgrimage every year. Thus, I had for several years desired to make the trip.

The traditional yatra (pilgrimage) reaches the cave every year on the Raksha-Bandhan Purnima (full moon) which comes near the end of August. I decided, however, as many do, to go one month earlier. After days of elaborate preparations, we finally left Srinagar for Pahalgam on the morning of 23rd July. The weather that day was very bad, which rather worried us, as the trip to the cave takes one over narrow and steep mountain paths which get very treacherous in the rain. Nevertheless, we set out with a determination to make the attempt even if it meant undergoing considerable inconvenience.

The holy cave of Amarnath beckons its devotees to a height of about 13,000 feet. It is 28 miles from Pahalgam, but small though this distance may seem on paper, in reality it is a very considerable trek. No vehicular traffic can go beyond Pahalgam, and the mountain path has to be traversed either on foot or on a horse. Due to a permanent disability caused by a series of mishaps several years ago it is not possible for me to ride or to walk long distances, particularly uphill. I was, therefore, obliged to be carried in a dandi, a makeshift chair carried by porters, much as I disliked having to use this form of transport.

After lunch at the charming Pahalgam Club we set off for our first camp, Chandanwari, which is 8 miles from Pahalgam. By now the rain had settled into a steady sharp drizzle, turning the earth into rich squelchy chocolate. The Lidder stream rushes and tumbles down the narrow valley and the path of Chandanwari leads up its right bank. We started at about three in the afternoon, the three ladies in the party, including my wife, insisting on walking despite the deep and slippery mud. I got into my dandi, carried by sturdy Kashmiri porters, and the rest of the party either rode or walked.

Luckily, the rain was not heavy enough to block out the lovely scenery that surrounded us as we trudged along. The sound of the stream, at first about a 100 yards below us on our right, had a soothing quality. Both sides of the valley were thickly wooded. After we had traversed the first 2 miles of the narrow and uneven path, the roar of the water grew louder and suddenly we emerged within a few yards of the stream. The water was rushing along, tripping over itself as if in a terrific hurry to get somewhere. Here the valley widened, and on either side the steep mountains were covered with green. The rich grass which swept almost to the summit, the tall pines and birches, the numerous varieties of shrubs and bushes all added their individual shade of green so that the whole scene looked like a vast green checkerboard curving up on both sides to the sky. Some stray cloudlets separated from their parent mass, ventured timorously down the mountain sides, only to get lost among the ridges.

As we proceeded, I threw my head back and closed my eyes. The swinging motion of the dandi and the continual roar of the stream combined to produce an almost hypnotic effect. I let my mind dwell upon the majestic figure of the great Lord Shiva sitting calm and inscrutable, lost in profound meditation. It is to the shrine of Mahadeva that I was going and I hummed one of the numerous songs composed in his glory.

After four hours of exhausting trekking, exhausting I may add not for me, being comfortably carried along, but for the porters and those who walked, we reached Chandanwari. Our camp had already been pitched and a hot cup of tea soon revived our spirits, somewhat dampened by the bad weather.

Before dinner we all got together in the dining tent and, joined by some of the other pilgrims also making the yatra, sang bhajans for about an hour. I greatly enjoyed these kirtans and we kept up these sessions regularly every evening during the yatra.

This was followed by a fairly substantial dinner, after which we all flopped gratefully into bed. Before turning in I noticed with trepidation that the sky was thickly overcast.

As soon as I woke the next day, at about seven, I jumped out of bed and threw open the flap of my tent. Bright sunlight streamed in and I looked out upon a clear blue sky. All traces of clouds had vanished. I was struck by the beauty of Chandanwari, which I had missed the previous day. Chandanwari is a small camping ground, about a square mile in area, situated at the bottom of a gigantic 'cup', the sides of which are deeply wooded mountains which tower against the sky. In the freshness of the morning sun, it was very beautiful.

After an early breakfast we set out for Sheshnag, our next destination, at 8 am. It is 7 miles from Chandanwari to Sheshnag, but the path was steep and treacherous. For about half a mile we followed the bank of the Lidder. Then we came to a murderous 2 mile climb known as Pissu Ghati, which rises about 2,000 feet above the river. The path was narrow and the turns sharp. In bad weather this incline becomes very dangerous and has claimed many victims. That day, however, the weather was fine, but nevertheless it was an exhausting climb.

A pilgrimage symbolizes, as it were, the long pilgrimage of the soul towards its supreme goal. Almost all the most important pilgrimages in India take the devotee along dangerous and hazardous paths in order to test his devotion. If he is deterred, it is seldom possible for him to reach the goal. If he pushes on bravely with courage, confidence, and faith in God he is bound to triumph.

It took the best part of two hours to negotiate Pissu Ghati. I must express my unbounded admiration for the porters who carried me up that slope. I tried walking a few yards but at that height—the climb rises from about 9,000 to about 11,000 feet—my heart started beating wildly. And yet these people carried me up that slope with apparent ease and without a single false step. Including the weight of the dandi they must have been carrying over 300 pounds.

There are many legends connected with the Amarnath yatra and the various places which one traverses during the pilgrimage. These legends are found in the *Amarkatha* which is a Sanskrit account of the pilgrimage, its origin and significance. This *Amarkatha* is believed to have been related by Lord Shiva himself to his consort Parvati in the Amarnath cave. There is an interesting legend regarding Pissu Ghati (actually Poushakhya Parvat): once the Devas and the Asuras were making their way up this mountain to pay homage to Mahadeva. On the way they quarrelled as to who should go first, and this resulted in a battle between them. The Devas got the worst of the battle and prayed desperately to Mahadeva for help. Mahadeva came to their rescue and destroyed the Asuras. The huge rocks and boulders which lie strewn on the slope represent the bodies of those demons. It is said that by climbing that mountain one's sins are destroyed by Mahadeva in the same manner as he destroyed the Asuras.

On reaching the top of the mountain we were rewarded by a lovely view. Far in the distance, Pahalgam nestled in the mountains. On all sides huge mountain peaks reared their hoary heads high into the air, while far below the Lidder was now a restless tape of silver, winding its way down to the plains. I stopped here for a quarter of an hour taking photographs and chatted with some sadhus who were making the pilgrimage.

From here on, for about 4 miles, there was a smooth decline along which we travelled at a fair pace. The scenery grew more spectacular and often I stopped and gazed in rapture at a breath-taking sight. At one place opposite us on the right a huge glacier rose to over 15,000 feet. From its gleaming snows, a stream drops like a luminous silver band down the sheer mountain side thousands of feet until it joins the Lidder at the bottom. On our side of the gorge the mountains were covered with green grass about three-quarters of the way up, ending in jagged rocks of a curious brick red colour of which different layers are distinctly visible. Above, a pair of magnificent eagles circle in majestic flight. A little further on I suddenly heard a most unusual shrill whistle and see, sitting on a rock about a 100 yards away, a small animal covered with reddish fur, which I recognized as a marmot. I saw many more of these little creatures as I went on.

We reached a height of about 12,000 feet, and abruptly the trees vanished, as we had passed the tree-line. From here on there was green grass and a variety of small green shrub, but not a single bush or tree.

We finished another stiff half-mile climb, at the top of which we suddenly came face to face with the lovely green lake of Sheshnag, about a mile long and a quarter of a mile broad, surmounted by a mighty glacier.

Soon the Sheshnag huts were in sight and we passed them

to proceed to our camping ground across the stream. To cross, we had to go over a bridge of solid ice under which the stream flowed. It looked as if it had been carved out of gigantic blocks of ivory. A few clouds came up, but they were white, fluffy, friendly clouds, so unlike the saturnine monsters that had scowled and rumbled at us yesterday. And the sun shone huge and friendly in the deep sky.

Our camp had been pitched on a lovely meadow overlooking the lake. I made my way to the top of a shallow incline and sat on a rock surveying the breathtaking view.

Before me was Sheshnag, its water a peculiar milky green colour. Behind it a huge glacier rose to three mighty peaks of snow and ice, as if symbolizing the divine trinity of Brahma the Creator, Vishnu the Preserver, and Mahadeva the Destroyer. To the right, the mass of a rocky mountain rose straight out of the lake. Behind me the distant grey rocks were covered with freshly fallen snow which, when melting, came down in a gushing stream culminating in a white waterfall.

The scene was both calming and inspiring. Its sedate beauty soothed the mind, restless from the cares and tribulations, the worries and sorrows of life. Its lofty peaks stood out against the deep blue sky and raised one's thoughts above the mundane into the pure realms of the spirit. One distinctly felt the underlying presence of a power greater, stronger, purer, than one's own petty self. For a while I glimpsed the lovely face of nature in its pure and undesecrated majesty. The torrent of time slackened, the problems and strifes of life paled into insignificance, and I was lost in deep contemplation.

I cherish a desire in the recesses of my heart to one day build myself a small ashrama in such surroundings where, with the body and mind made pure and free from the grasping tentacles of desire and fear, ego and attachment, I could concentrate upon the unalloyed purity of nature and thereby perhaps achieve spiritual illumination. If the day comes when I am able to fulfil this desire, then I can think of no better spot than where I was sitting, overlooking that placid lake.

The legend runs that at one time a mighty Asura lived among these mountains who, in the form of a terrifying whirlwind, wrought great havoc among the Devas. In distress they went to Shiva, but he said that he had given the Asura a boon not to kill him. He advised them to go to Lord Vishnu. Then the Devas went to the bank of the lake Sheshnag and prayed to Vishnu, singing songs to His Glory. Pleased, Lord Vishnu arose from the Lake seated upon the back of the mighty serpent, the thousand-headed Sheshnag. 'O King of Serpents' they said, 'with your thousand mouths destroy this Asura.' Upon hearing this command Sheshnag fell upon the Asura and destroyed him. From that day the lake and the mountain behind it have been known as Sheshnag.

With reluctance I dragged myself back to the camp for lunch. After a short rest I went to see how my fellow pilgrims were faring. A group of about a dozen ash-besmeared sadhus had seated themselves on a small knoll quite near our camp and I went over and chatted with them. They are a curious race, these sadhus. Some are men of great spiritual achievements, but alas, some have made it a profession to live upon the religious susceptibilities of us Indians, particularly Indian women. Sheshnag is at about 13,000 feet above sea level, and at that height all of us were feeling rather breathless and oppressed. I walked briskly to the main Sheshnag camp, then I returned and distributed warm clothing and rations to those pilgrims who needed them. By now it was evening, and we all gathered in a tent to hear a pandit read to us from the *Amarkatha,* followed by kirtan.

By the time we finished the kirtan it was nine, and quite dark. An almost full moon hung luminously between the mountain peaks. I walked up the small incline to see the lake by moonlight. In the day, the lake has an air of mystery and haunting beauty, but by night this effect is greatly enhanced. Sheshnag lies calm and deep, the moonlight mirrored on half its surface. The other half lies in the dark shadow of the mountains which rise behind it, bathed in mystic light. Time stood still in this enchanted moonlit panorama, and one felt in harmony with the deeper currents of pure Existence.

Once again I reluctantly came back to the camp where a simple though ample dinner awaited us. I may add that from the time we left Srinagar to the day we returned our diet was strictly vegetarian, as is customary on a yatra. After dinner we retired to bed, though at that height sleep was difficult and not sound.

I awoke the next morning at five, and immediately struggled to get out from under the masses of blankets which had kept me warm at night. To my surprise it was already fairly light. I could not resist the temptation to again visit my favourite spot. I had seen the lake by daylight and by moonlight. Now I wanted to see it in what is the most pleasant and also—excepting dusk—the most mysterious time of day. I walked to the top of the hill and was rewarded as before with a remarkable view. This time a fresh delightful morning breeze played on my face and hands. The lake and the mountains looked pale and the trinity of peaks seemed immersed in deep meditation. I felt a great joy rise in my heart and could not restrain myself from singing out aloud. First, I sang Shankaracharya's six stanzas in Sanskrit portraying the highest *Advaita* (Monistic) philosophy, each stanza ending with the words 'Chidenanda Rupa Shivoham Shivoham' (My form is pure bliss, I am Shiva, I am Shiva). Then I sang a few bhajans in those delightful morning ragas, Bhairav and Todi.

Just as I finished my last song the first ray of sunlight struck the top of the central peak with a shaft of gold. The peak flushed, as if with joy to feel the warm caress of the sun. Slowly the sunlight covered the three peaks and moved down the mountain side. Soon the golden orb of the sun itself peeped over the mountains in the east and a warm glow of well-being spread over the whole area.

I descended to the camp and bathed. It is considered very auspicious to bathe in the Sheshnag lake, and several of the braver members of our party went down about half a mile to the lake to do so. I have to admit that I used the less orthodox, though certainly more convenient, method of getting water from the lake carried up and warmed it for my bath. After breakfast we all set off for our next destination, Panchtarni, which is 8 miles from Sheshnag.

The holy road to Amarnath has through the centuries been trodden by lakhs of pilgrims. I felt a reverential awe when I considered how many men of great spiritual stature must have passed over the track along which my dandi was now swinging. Many giants, unknown and unsung, must have trodden this very same path. Along this path, the great Swami Vivekananda, back from his triumphant 'conquest' of America, travelled in 1898 to pay homage to Amarnath. Swami Ramtirath also made this pilgrimage. Along this route, over a thousand years earlier, Swami Shankaracharya, one of the most brilliant and profound intellects India has produced, is reputed to have wound his way towards the shrine of the other Shankara.

Sheshnag itself, as I have said, is at about 13,000 feet but before us loomed another formidable climb, the Mahagunas mountain. For three miles we climbed slowly and breathlessly. The scenery around us was beautiful. To the left of us rose the huge mountain, while to the right, hundreds of feet below, the stream grew smaller and smaller. On the mountain side the grass swept right up to the skyline, covered with thousands of delicate little buttercups making a quivering carpet of yellow. Below, near the stream there were flat green spaces across which impudent marmots scampered, whistling in glee. All around, mighty glaciers and rocky peaks loomed into the morning sky.

Higher and higher rose the path, until at last we reached the top of the Mahagunas Pass, about 15,000 feet high. There we dismounted and took photographs and movies of the magnificent panorama of glaciers that surrounded us. Patches of snow lay around us, and a few wisps of white cloud floated across the sky.

From here the descent started, a long 5 mile decline to Panchtarni. The scenery was rugged, and the stern barren mountains possessed an impressive beauty. There were no trees at this height, and the only greenery was the grass which grows even at the highest points. The mountains that were nearly bare had a powder grey colour. In the distance Amarnath rose to about 18,000 feet. It is in this mountain that the holy cave is situated.

On the descent we picked up speed and my dandi swung briskly along, while I divided my time between surveying the view and reading Paul Brunton's fascinating *Search in Secret India*. We stopped at several places to stretch our legs and take photographs. Fresh mountain streams flowed downwards past our feet to the river. Some of these came from melting snows hundreds of feet above, others emerged startlingly from dry ground. These latter apparently flow underground for some distance before rising up into the sunlight. Several times I heard the shrill whistle of the marmots, but failed to locate any of the little brown beasts. I wanted to catch a pair of young marmots and try and tame them as pets, but they are reputed to be very difficult to catch alive as they always stay near their holes, into which they dive indignantly if anyone approaches.

At last, the Panchtarni plain came into sight. Here, it is said, once long ago, Lord Shiva was performing the Tandava Nritya (the cosmic dance of destruction). He was so immersed in ecstasy that while dancing, his massive locks became undone and from them five streams of the Ganga fell to the ground. These five streams (Panchtarangini) are considered to be very sacred and bathing in them very auspicious. The Panchtarni plain is about a mile long and over a quarter of a mile broad. A stream flows through it which is joined by four other streams coming down from the mountains with barren angular crags. To the east is a large glacier, the snow of which has been shaped, presumably by the wind, into curious crater-like formations which I had not seen anywhere else. Through binoculars these looked very like craters on the moon.

The weather remained perfect. Occasionally, a small cloud would drift between the sun and us, and then suddenly the temperature would drop considerably and we would begin to shiver. But almost immediately a friendly breeze would blow the offending cloud away and we would once again be in the comforting warmth of the sun.

After lunch and a short nap, I wandered off on an exploratory stroll around the camp. Invisible marmots shrieked at my approach but search as I would, I could not locate a single one of these elusive little animals. I walked to the foot of a small waterfall on the mountain behind our camp. I was struck by the profusion of small wild flowers that grew everywhere. In one place, within a square yard, I counted seven different types of flowers all of different colours. Many rare herbs also grow upon these uninhabited mountains. Some, I am told, extremely valuable. There were also lovely stones lying about, some delicately veined, others sparkling in the sun with mica.

In the evening we had the usual kirtan. Singing at that height is quite exhausting, and after each song one felt breathless. After that we had dinner and retired to bed early, as the next day was the culminating point of our pilgrimage with a visit to the holy cave of Amarnath.

I was woken at five the next morning with shouts of 'Shree Amarnath Swami ki Jai,' outside my tent. Devout pilgrims were already on their way to the cave. It was so cold that I snuggled under my blankets for another hour before venturing out. We were all ready by eight and set out for the cave with a feeling of expectation and excitement. As is the tradition, I did not have anything at all to eat and drink until after I had visited the cave.

The path to the cave leads out of Panchtarni and goes round the mountain at the base of which our camp was pitched. For a few 100 yards it goes along the stream, then it curves and rapidly goes higher. The bends were very steep and sharp and some of them were quite unnerving, particularly as the path was narrow and the loose earth gave way under one's feet. Soon we were at a dizzy height and still climbing higher. In several places I just closed my eyes and hoped for the best when we negotiated the twists.

Higher and higher we climbed for about 3 miles. The mighty Amarnath mountain rose in front of us. High on its grass-covered slopes, just a few 100 feet below the rocky summit, we saw goats and horses grazing—black specks moving calmly on the precarious mountainside. These animals belonged to Bakkarwals, those bearded nomads who in winter came down to the plains but in summer moved up to grazing places such as these. The Bakkarwals' tents were also pitched up there. To see them was enough to make one quite dizzy. And, if those animals took one false step they would have fallen a sheer 2000 feet to their pulpy doom. But instinct, often a surer guide than even human intelligence, did not fail them, and they retained their foothold with ease.

After climbing for about three miles there was a sudden turn to the right and we began to descend rapidly. Soon we came to the bottom of a narrow steep ravine, only about 150 yards broad, whose gigantic cliffs loomed hundreds of precipitous feet to the skyline. For about half a mile we had to travel over solid ice. Soon the famous cave of Amarnath came into sight, a huge cavity in the mountain. We went on almost to the end of the ravine, where about 50 yards below the cave, a tent had been pitched for us.

To the left of the cave the Amaravati stream flows down from the mountain. This is a very sacred stream and devotees are expected to bathe in it and smear their bodies with its mud before entering the cave. Here again, I adopted the unorthodox course of getting the water carried in buckets to the tent, but this time I did not get it warmed up and instead bathed with the ice cold water. It was a clear and warm day, however, so the cold bath did not cause any inconvenience. At that height the sun is very warm, and somehow looked bigger than when seen from lower ground. We all got badly sunburnt as a result. After the bath I emerged from the tent clad only in a yellow dhoti, and then climbed up the steep path to the cave.

Margaret Noble, better known as Sister Nivedita, in her *Notes of Some Wanderings with the Swami Vivekananda* describes the visit of the Swami to this sacred cave, 'The place was vast, large enough to hold a Cathedral, and the great ice-Shiva, in a niche of deepest shadow, sacred as if throned on its own base.' She recorded that Swami Vivekananda was so overwhelmed when he entered the cave that his whole frame shook and he almost swooned with emotion. 'I have enjoyed it so much,' the Swami said later, 'I thought the ice-lingam was Shiva himself. And there were no thievish Brahmans, no trade, nothing wrong. It was all worship. I never enjoyed any religious place so much.' Afterwards he would tell of an overwhelming mystical experience that came to him in the cave, in which Shiva himself appeared before him and granted him the boon of Amarnath, the Lord of Immortality, not to die until he himself should choose to throw off his mortal bonds. He would also talk of the poetry of the white ice pillar, and suggested that the place had been first discovered by a party of shepherds who, wandering far in search of their flocks, had one summer day entered the cave to find themselves, before the 'unmelting' ice, in the presence of the Lord Himself.

The cave is of truly colossal dimensions. Its outer mouth must measure about 40 yards across, and it is about 75 feet high and at least 80 feet deep sloping down into the mountain side. Inside, a central ice formation rising to about 5 feet and ending in a glistening cone, represents Lord Shiva. To the right is a block of pure white ice, about 6 feet high and 3 feet in diameter which represents Ganesha, while to the left is a smaller ice formation representing Shiva's consort Parvati. These ice formations, which form during the summer months, are believed to wax and wane along with the moon, reaching their climax on the full moon day and vanishing completely on moonless days.

The cave is one of the most sacred spots in all India. As I entered I suddenly had the curious feeling that I had been there before. The cave certainly has a very unusual atmosphere which powerfully affects many people. I felt quite overawed as I entered its hallowed precincts. Before the ice lingam of Shiva, my wife and I performed the traditional puja and made offerings of cash, cloth, and dried fruit. Then with folded hands we all sang a hymn to Lord Shiva. The same procedure was repeated before the symbols of Ganesh and Parvati, where offerings were also made.

The traditional method of distribution of these offerings is interesting. No one stays permanently at the cave, so after the pilgrims have made their offerings these are collected by the camp officer, a Government official who accompanies the pilgrimage. These offerings, both in cash and kind, are divided into three equal portions. One portion goes to the Mahant of the pilgrimage, who resides at Srinagar. The second goes to the Pandas (priests) of Mattan, another place of pilgrimage 20 miles short of Pahalgam. The third portion goes to a Muslim family of Mallicks, who also live near Pahalgam. Representatives of these three beneficiaries accompanied us to the cave to be sure that they were not deprived of their share of the offerings.

After the puja was over we emerged from the cave into the bright sunlight. It was chilly in the cave and, in my thin dhoti, I was shivering. Outside the cave we saw the famous pair of rock pigeons who stay near the cave throughout the year, even in the winter when not a blade of grass is visible. The legend is that these were two followers of Lord Shiva who once disturbed him during his meditation. In anger Shiva turned them into pigeons, who now always live near him in the cave. It is curious that these pigeons have been seen for scores of years, seemingly with a much longer lifespan than a normal pigeon. Whether they are the same pigeons, in some mysterious way, replaced when they die is impossible to say.

We descended again to the tent where a freshly cooked lunch awaited us, after which I lay down for a while. By now the cave was completely deserted and I walked up again. This time I got a very good view of the inside of the cave, without the crowds, and the ice formations, which are truly remarkable.

It is with reluctance that I left the cave. Some undefinable attraction made the parting a poignant one. The gleaming ice lingam possesses a strange power of attraction and I drew myself away with some difficulty.

We negotiated the return journey to Panchtarni at a brisk speed, and were back in camp by six. After the usual kirtan I retired to bed with a feeling of peace and satisfaction.

We left Panchtarni early next morning, as we planned to reach Chandanwari in the evening and had to negotiate two laps instead of one. As the dandi swung along I again felt a strange pang, as if I was leaving behind some dearly loved friend. I turned to get a last glimpse of the Amarnath mountain and in my mind paid silent homage to the Lord of Amarnath.

We started the long tedious 5 mile climb to the top of the Mahagunas. On the way we passed to our right a place known as Hatyara Talao (the tank of Death) where one year forty pilgrims met their death in an avalanche which their own loud hymns had started. That route is now banned, as it is very hazardous.

Once we got to the top of the mountain, the porters speeded up and we were in Sheshnag by noon. Immediately, I made my way to my favourite spot overlooking the lake with the three lofty pinnacles of aged snow.

After lunch we set off again, as we were keen to get past the formidable Pissu Ghati before dark. As my dandi travelled along the path, about 500 hundred feet above Sheshnag, I felt an irresistible desire to go down to the shore of the lake. Half way down I suddenly heard the call of a marmot very close and turning a corner saw one standing on its hind legs just twenty feet from us. It was very cute and I got in several feet of film before it disappeared into its hole. We went down to the edge of the lake and drank from its ice cold water. The lake is very deep, its water falling to many feet almost immediately from the edge.

We walked along the shore and came upon a rock upon which an image of a seven-headed serpent, representing Sheshnag, was carved. Finally, we made our way back to the path after climbing laboriously and precariously up the hill.

The weather for the fourth day in succession remained beautifully clear. One among our party was an incorrigible prophet of doom, always prophesying bad weather, landslides, and other dire calamities. Fortunately for us all, however, the weather was as good as it could possibly have been. I certainly would not have cherished having to negotiate Pissu Ghati and those other precarious inclines in bad weather. As soon as the corner shutting out the view of Sheshnag was turned, trees began to reappear and grew denser as we progressed towards Chandanwari. At last, we arrived again at Pissu Ghati. But by now I had complete confidence in the porters, who negotiated the steep descent with ease. We got into Chandanwari just before sunset, where, after kirtan and dinner, we retired for the night. The next morning, after distributing well-earned rewards among the porters, pony men, and others who had helped to make the pilgrimage the success that it was, we set off for Pahalgam on the last lap of our trip back to Srinagar. The Lidder, still retaining the green colour derived from its mother lake, rushed along through its gorge. Lovely little birds sang merrily, flitting from tree to tree. At one place a monkey sat on a rock, watching us with sedate surprise.

News of my return must have travelled in advance, as in several places Gujjars had collected to greet me, their women singing pahari songs of welcome. The Gujjars are a semi-nomadic tribe who keep large herds of buffaloes and every year travel down to the plains. Their songs have much in common with the lilting Dogra hill songs.

On the way I chatted with the porters. One of them, an old man with a soft face, full of unlettered wisdom, gave me his simple philosophy of life. 'Sarkar,' he said, 'Khuda helps those who are patient. Difficulties and troubles come but one must bear them with patience and faith in god. Take this pilgrimage. On the first day it rained heavily and there was much discomfort. If you had been disheartened and turned back, the pilgrimage would have failed. But you had faith in god and pushed on. The result was that the pilgrimage was a great success.'

Soon we reached the village of Pahalgam. Outside the first house, a tiny Kashmiri boy, wearing only a little shirt, stood waiting eagerly. As soon as my dandi passed him he ran screaming with delight into the arms of the foremost porter, who was evidently his father. It was a heart-warming little incident.

In Pahalgam, we made our way to the club and sat upon a wooden terrace overlooking the swiftly flowing river. 'O Lidder,' I mused, 'I have seen your birthplace amidst the mighty three-peaked glacier. I have seen you gush down its snow clad slopes into green Sheshnag, only to emerge broader and more powerful. I have followed your twists and turns, your pools and rapids, down the narrow valley, and now you will gurgle on till at last you mingle with the slow flowing waters of the broad Jhelum.'

After lunch I paid a quick visit to two local temples, and then drove off for Srinagar. As the car passed between lines of poplars, flanked by smiling fields of maize and paddy, my thoughts returned again and again to the holy cave. How remote, how impenetrable those lofty mountains had seemed, how hazardous the steep and narrow path. Yet once at the cave what peace and serenity descended upon one. Thus, I venture to hope, after I have crossed the steep mountains and deep gorges of life, a deep and eternal peace awaits me.

EAST AND SOUTH INDIA
(1954)

Through my life, I have kept occasional diaries about my inner quest and find that they are full of such references: 'What is this mystic experience about which all the saints have written through the ages as being one of absolute bliss and unadulterated joy? But how? How?' And again: 'I wonder when I shall also reach a stage of spiritual development in which I also might come into direct and intimate contact with the Lord of the Sacrifice, the Knower of the Field'—these terms are taken, of course, from the teachings of Lord Krishna in the Bhagavad Gita.

These urgings were stimulated largely by Romain Rolland's *Life of Vivekananda*, Sri Aurobindo's *Synthesis of Yoga,* and Paramahansa Yogananda's *Autobiography of a Yogi*. I was doing my daily puja regularly, but although it gave me strength it did not bring any of the mystic visions that so many seekers had experienced. However, my dreams became, and remain, extremely rich in psychic material. Indeed, ever since my early twenties I have been having the most extraordinary dreams night after night, sometimes several in quick succession. It was only some years later after I had met Sri Krishnaprem that I realized that dreams, if properly interpreted, can provide valuable clues to one's psychic and psychological problems and to the manner in which the multiple crises of life can be surmounted.

The great appeal of Hinduism, of course, lies in its infinite diversity which caters to people with different psychological and spiritual backgrounds. Instead of trying to steamroll everyone into exactly the same formula or mode of worship, it allows the seeker a choice not only between a personal and a formless divinity, but between different aspects and images of the divine. Our family deity is Sri Rama, whose great temple in Jammu built by Maharaja Ranbir Singh is surely one of the finest in India. The main shrine is surrounded by a quadrangle which has 1,25,000 shaligrams, stones from the bed of sacred streams, then by a larger quadrangle with many temples containing images of almost all the major figures in the Hindu pantheon, and then again by the outer quadrangle which has Shiva temples enshrining the ashes of my ancestors. I have recently added to this a Nataraja temple, the first in north India, which has a lead crystal Shivalingam fabricated in Germany under which, in due course, some of my own and my wife's ashes will be placed.

But it was to Krishna that I was more drawn. Towards the end of 1953, after we had moved down from Jammu for the winter, I recorded in my diary: 'I have as yet not settled down to any one path or any one particular deity. Of course, God is omnipresent, but nevertheless it is a help if one worships one particular aspect of Him. I am beginning to get greatly attached to the wonderful form of the divine Lord Krishna, and a deep and emotional love for him is beginning to grow in my being...I am now keenly awaiting some initiation into some form of yoga whereby I might really and truly set out upon the path of spiritual illumination.'

It was perhaps in search of such illumination that shortly thereafter I set out on an extended pilgrimage to east and south India. The quest for spiritual enlightenment has traditionally been linked in India with travel to various shrines situated in distant parts of the country. Until then, except for Punjab, Dehra Dun, Delhi, and Bombay, I had hardly seen anything of India because I had been largely confined to my own state. Asha and I first visited my mother in the Kangra valley where she had rented a beautiful palace belonging to the Nawab of Bahawalpur at a place called Alhilal between Palampur and Baijnath, which had been declared evacuee property. With her we went up to Mandi and Suket, small hill states in Himachal, which have a great deal in common culturally with the Jammu region, and also visited Riwalsar, a place sacred to both Hindus and Buddhists, which has a lake where small islands float around mysteriously. Then we proceeded to Calcutta, where I was astonished to see for the first time such vast numbers of people concentrated in a single city, more people than in the whole of Jammu and Kashmir.

We went to the great Kali temple at Dakshineshwar where Sri Ramakrishna, one of the most remarkable religious figures in history, had lived as the temple priest in the middle of the 19th century and had, through his astounding spiritual experiences, triggered a virtual revolution within Hinduism at a time when a spiritual and intellectual crisis was sweeping across the land. I had read a good deal about him and his leading disciple Narendranath Datta, better known as Swami Vivekananda, who carried the teachings of his master not only through the length and breadth of India but also to the Western world. I was fascinated by Vivekananda's personality, his glowing eloquence and leonine mien. The visit to Dakshineshwar was a moving experience, and on the return drive we went to the Belur Math, where Vivekananda founded the Ramakrishna Mission which carries on his work to this day. We also paid a visit to Kalighat, from which Calcutta derives its name, and there we saw the goddess in her terrifying form. Terrifying, that is, for the evil-doers; for her devotees she remains the divine mother to whom so much of Hindu devotion is directed.

The visit to Calcutta only whetted my appetite for exploring the rest of India, and in 1954 I embarked on a long tour of the south including visits to many famous shrines. My mother, who had always yearned to do a yatra like this, also came with us along with her elder brother Thakur Nachint Chand and some servants. By the time we set off it was quite a large party, and so we decided to go by train. It was truly a memorable visit for me, opening up aspects of our cultural heritage of which we in the north were hardly aware.

Here was the Hindu tradition in its pristine glory; the great temple Gopurams soaring into the sky covered with their incredible carvings often brightly painted; the richly caparisoned temple elephants, and the priests who received us at each of the great temples and conducted us through those massive monuments until we reached the inner sanctum where the main deity is installed; the haunting notes of the Karnataka music, so different from the north Indian mode and yet in some ways richer and more profound; the rhythmic, almost hypnotic chanting of Sanskrit prayers in unison, bringing out the glory of this greatest of languages in a deeply devotional setting: all combined to leave an indelible impression upon me. To this day I find myself attracted to the south, almost as if there was a spiritual link reaching far back into the recesses of time.

We visited the great Meenakshi temple in Madurai, dedicated to the fish-eyed goddess, and the Brihadishwara temple in Thanjavur with its huge Shivalingam, probably the most impressive temple in the whole of India. We saw the famous Shiva temple in Tiruvannamalai and visited the nearby ashram of Ramana Maharshi, one of the greatest saints of our times, who had passed away in 1950. We also saw the celebrated temple at Chidambaram where Shiva is worshipped in the form of the Divine Dancer, the Nataraja, one of the great artistic creations of mankind. We went to the temple of Srirangam in Tiruchirapalli, an entire town in itself, which we happened to reach on an especially auspicious day of the year, Vaikuntha Ekadashi, when the great northern gate is opened. We also went down to Rameshwaram, one of the four main pilgrim centres in the corners of India consecrated by Adi Shankaracharya, the remarkable 8th-century philosopher saint who did so much for the regeneration of Hinduism and the spiritual unity of India. There Sri Rama, the hero of the

Ramayana and for millions of Hindus, god incarnate, had worshipped Shiva before setting out for Lanka, where his wife Sita was held captive by the demon king Ravana.

After the temples in Tamil Nadu, we proceeded further south to Kerala and went right down to Kanya Kumari, the tip of India where three great oceans meet. There we saw the small, exquisite temple dedicated to the Virgin Goddess, and a few miles away a huge statue of Hanuman at Suchindram. In Trichur we visited the famous Shiva temple built in the typical Kerala style of architecture, smaller and neater than the Tamil temples but in some ways even more appealing. As I visited these great shrines, redolent with myth and tradition yet vibrant with living devotion and uplifting ritual, it became clear to me that Hinduism was much richer than I had imagined. Here was the great reservoir of our culture and tradition, and I realized then that we in the north owe an undying debt of gratitude to south India for having preserved this great heritage intact down the troubled centuries.

A special revelation was my introduction to Bharatanatyam, the unique dance-form based on Bharata's *Natya Shastra* which embodies the highest reaches of artistic achievement. Combining bhava (emotion), raga (melody), and tala (rhythm), the Bharatanatyam is the world's most impressive solo dance form. We were in Madras when we saw it for the first time with Vyjayanthimala performing in the Music Academy. I was stunned by the combination of swift movements and statuesque poses which she presented in a virtually continuous three-hour programme, at once deeply sensuous and spiritually inspiring. Ever since I have been a devotee of the dance, and have had the privilege of seeing many great artistes, including Balasaraswati and Yamini Krishnamurty, whom I consider outstanding dancers in their respective generations.

During this visit we also went to Pondicherry, as I was becoming interested in the philosophy of that remarkable patriot philosopher Sri Aurobindo and wanted to meet his spiritual collaborator Madame Alfassa. The Mother, as she was universally called, received us with great courtesy at her residence. I am afraid my mother was not terribly impressed by her, but felt a certain strange presence which bespoke unusual psychic power. I was to see her twice again before she passed away many years later, but it was Sri Aurobindo, whom I never saw in the flesh, who fascinated me. His fervent nationalism and mastery over the English language, soaring spiritual vision and comprehensive philosophy made a deep impression upon me.

The cumulative effect on my mind of this south Indian tour was considerable. It not only gave me a deeper awareness of Hinduism's many-splendored dimensions, but also led me to realize that India was much richer and more varied than I had imagined, and that despite its bewildering diversity it was Hindu culture that provided the unifying motif, the great backdrop, as it were, to our long and eventful history. While I did not meet a guru on this trip, it helped sharpen my awareness of the spiritual dimension which had, over the preceding years, been overshadowed by political events and activity. At the same time, I began to realize that I did not want to be indefinitely confined to one corner of India, even though that corner was as beautiful as Kashmir.

HARIDWAR AND BEYOND
(Early 1970s)

Haridwar has been a sacred spot as far back as our history reaches, and the Ganga here is considered specially auspicious. On one of my visits to this town, we reached Haridwar by 6 pm, and spent the evening mingling with the pilgrims who thronged the bathing ghats listening to taped bhajans. Many younger people and children were swimming, while the elders performed arati and floated tiny diyas, earthenware lamps, down the river which twinkled like stars on the dark bosom of the Ganga. The clock tower was the main point where pilgrims gathered, and the whole scene reminded me somehow of St. Mark's Square in Venice, except that there the atmosphere of devotion is not as much in evidence.

We stayed in a Haveli built by my ancestors over a century ago which commands a magnificent view of the Ganga. Across the river, a series of low hills give the first faint promise of the great Himalayas that lie ahead. The clock tower struck determinedly throughout the night, out of tune except for the actual chimes, and one prayed that it could be turned off so that sleep or meditation could continue undisturbed. The children slept in the verandah, and looking up I was able, within half an hour, to spot three satellites making their way with majestic instancy across the star-spangled sky. It was remarkably cool at night, and we had to unroll our bedding and get out blankets. I am a prolific dreamer, and had several dreams including one where a Sufi asked me three questions to which I responded with a single indignant counter-question for which he seemed to have no answer.

Before going to sleep I had been reading from T.S. Eliot, and the deep impress of Hindu thought upon his writings was very evident. Indeed, the *Four Quartets* and *The Waste Land* are virtually contemporary Upanishads. Take, for example, these lines from 'Burnt Norton':

> *At the still point of the turning world. neither flesh nor fleshless;*
> *Neither from nor towards; at the still point, there the dance is.*

And *The Waste Land* actually concludes with the classical Upanishadic ending: 'Shantih, Shantih, Shantih.'

Later, we had a great deal of trouble with one of our cars, which delayed our departure from Haridwar and also slowed down our movement towards Srinagar. The first important spot en route was Rishikesh, where we went to the famous Lakshman Jhoola that swings across the Ganga. We were struck by the horrifying sight of sick people of different ages and genders afflicted with leprosy, shunned by society, living by the roadside. Their suffering and rejection was a symbol of a deep social malaise.

I walked across Lakshman Jhoola with my sons, and recalled doing so when I was about their age. The bridge actually swings when one walks on it, and provides a dramatic crossing of the Ganga. Monkeys on the way determinedly snatched packets of food from the boys' hands. In the middle of the bridge I was suddenly confronted by three young photographers who wanted to know if I was 'Dr. Karan Singh'. Although sorely tempted to pretend otherwise, it was not easy to lie standing directly above the sacred Ganga, and my carefully nurtured disguise collapsed ignominiously.

We drove on from Rishikesh, but the car kept breaking down en route and I reverted to Eliot. This time it was *Murder in the Cathedral*, in which Eliot is at his dramatic best. The following lines spoken by Archbishop Thomas Beckett struck a responsive chord:

Now is my way clear, now is the meaning plain
Temptation shall not come in this kind again.
The last temptation is the greatest treason
To do the right deed for the wrong reason…
I know that history at all times draws
The strangest consequences from remotest cause.

Reading the play, I was struck with how similar political conflicts are in every age and every country. Somehow politics seems to bring out the less noble qualities in human nature; intrigue, internecine conflicts, pressure groups jockeying for power, a lack of commitment to ideals, and a total subordination of means to ends seem to be a constant feature in political life throughout the world. A few great thinkers have from time to time sought to introduce higher values into the political system, and in our own country Sri Aurobindo and Mahatma Gandhi provided excellent examples of men with deep vision grappling with the problems of politics. However, the point arises as to how abiding the actual impact of such ideas is upon the body politic, and this brings one to the broader question of whether politics can be squared with the spiritual quest. Or, to put it differently, is it possible for a person whose main interest is the pursuit of the spiritual quest to take an active and effective part in politics? Although the evidence of history would seem to give us a negative answer, I pin my hopes in the exhortation of Krishna to Arjuna on the battlefield of Kurukshetra, in particular, the famous shloka in which he says:

> *By dedicating one's work to the Power who is the source of all activity, and by whom the universe is pervaded, man attains to perfection.*

Also, the clear objective of political activity mentioned in the Gita is *Lokasangraha*, the holding together of the peoples, and so if the field of work one has chosen is politics, and if it is pursued with the detachment and dedication that Krishna demands, there is no reason to treat politics as inherently inferior or unsuitable.

Our road continued through arid mountains, depressing in

their dry and unattractive appearance. In ancient days these would have been covered by thick forests, and indeed it was in such foothills of the Himalayas that the Vedic culture was born and flourished in such glory. The dreadful deforestation symbolizes not only spiritual aridity but, more concretely, the grave damage that has been done to the environment by the unthinking and unwise intervention of man. Throughout our five-day trip in the mountains, we did not see a single sign of wild life, and this in areas which only half a century ago were described by Jim Corbett as teeming with wild life of all types, including his celebrated man-eaters. I found this total absence of wild animals most tragic.

We entered Garhwal where Corbett spent many years and where his name is still a legend. Instead of man-eaters, however, there were children begging all along the way. It seemed that they had been taught by their parents to beg, because whenever any car passed they would mechanically thrust out their hands and chant *pai-paisa*, *pai-aisa*. It is a sobering thought that so many years after independence our future citizens should be begging on the roadside instead of being at school preparing themselves for the future. If there is any area where a well-organized social reform movement is required it is in these backward regions of Uttarakhand.

We finally reached Srinagar in the late afternoon. This is a much smaller town than its namesake in Kashmir, and is situated on the banks of the Alaknanda river. It was past five and we were all famished. After a quick meal at 'Menaka Hotel' opposite the road from our Rest House, we set out to explore the area and finally located the ancient Shiva temple nearby. This is the famous Kamaleshwara temple where Vishnu is believed to have worshipped Shiva for many centuries. Close by we discovered a Lakshmi Narayana temple run by a local *Math*. In the dim light a priest was reading from some text while a tiny girl stood by with folded hands. This temple is of some architectural importance and is in an excellent state of preservation. From there we went down to the river where the children paddled in the river.

Water in all its manifestations has a strange impact upon the human psyche, and in particular rushing torrents have held for me a strange fascination. The movement of the water, as well as its sound, combine to create a hypnotic effect in which one is lifted away from mundane levels of consciousness on to a different dimension. Ever since I was a child in Kashmir I have sought every available opportunity to sit on the banks of rivers. In a way they are symbolic of man's spiritual quest also because, despite all difficulties and obstacles, they ultimately merge with the great ocean. Indeed, the Buddhists have a term to describe a person's taking to the spiritual path; they call it 'entering the stream'.

We returned to our lodgings and fell asleep to the silvery notes of a flute someone was playing deep into the night.

***

The drive from Rishikesh to Badrinath takes one past five different confluences, or *prayags*, symbolic of the great quality of synthesis that has been the hallmark of Indian civilization through the ages. The first, Deo Prayag, is the confluence of the Alaknanda and the Bhagirathi rivers. The second is Rudra Prayag, some kilometres beyond Srinagar, where the Alaknanda and the Mandakani rivers join, and it is from here that the road to Kedarnath branches off. Unfortunately, time did not permit us to visit Kedarnath this time, and as we passed the turning I was reminded of Robert Frost's 'The Road Not Taken':

Two roads diverged in a yellow wood,
And sorry I could not travel both
And be one traveller, long I stood
And looked down one as far as I could,
To where it bent in the undergrowth.
Then took the other, as just as fair
And having perhaps the better claim
Because it was grassy and wanted wear,
Though as for that the passing there
Had worn them really about the same.

I shall be telling this with a sigh,
Somewhere ages and ages hence,
Two roads diverged in a wood, and I,
I took the one less travelled by,
And that has made all the difference.

Two roads confront one throughout life's journey. The *Katha Upanishad* mentions the *shreya* (good) and *preya* (pleasant). Moments come in life when one is confronted with a choice between two options, and the road one takes leads on to a new direction which steadily diverges from the other. It is at these critical moments in our destiny that our intuition, intellect, and emotions must work in close harmony if the correct path is to be chosen.

Speaking of the Upanishads, I am struck by an interesting comparison between them and the Bhagavad Gita. The Upanishads are scriptures of forest ashramas where the teacher and the disciples are together in an atmosphere of sylvan calm and harmonious natural surroundings. The Gita, on the other hand, is essentially the scripture of the battlefield. Here the teacher and the disciple are meeting amidst the sound of conches and the flight of missiles. Again, whereas the Upanishads speak of the ultimate reality as a great impersonal power, in the Gita this reality is personified in Krishna and there is an immediacy of contact between him and Arjuna which is very moving.

Making the journey along with us, or returning from the pilgrimage, were a number of sadhus of various ages, shapes, and sizes. It is extraordinary how these people wander around the entire country without any material possessions, and yet seem to survive without starvation. Many of them are people who have given up an affluent life to take to the path of the wandering mendicant; others have opted out of the mainstream because of frustration or some personal tragedy. In a way the life of the sadhu has provided through the centuries a valuable escape mechanism in Hindu society for those unwilling or unable to adjust to the demands of the existing social order.

The hippy phenomenon in the West of the 1960s is very similar, and there is a lot in common between them and the sadhus, whether it is their long hair and beards, their clothing or their proclivity for smoking pot. This is not to denigrate the fact that many among the sadhus and, for that matter, the hippies, are people who are seriously trying to pursue their spiritual destiny.

The road from Rudra Prayag winds onwards towards that next confluence at Karan Prayag. The figure of my distinguished name-sake, the tragic hero of the *Mahabharata*, has fascinated me since my childhood, and I was looking forward to seeing Karan Prayag, where the Pindar river comes rushing down from the Pindari glacier to mingle dramatically with the Alaknanda. I visited the temple of Uma Devi and Raja Karan close to the junction. It was in a wretched condition, despite a beautiful black stone statue of Shiva about 3 feet high and several others indistinguishable in the semi-darkness. I promised myself to send them a proper statue of Karan which the pujari said would be most welcome.

Resuming our drive, we came upon a sadhu whose legs had been amputated and who was making the trip on a hand-operated tricycle. We learnt from him that he had for the last fourteen years been travelling to various holy places of India in this fashion. We were moved by his courage, and he exuded a sense of dignified calm which was impressive. As the road wound onwards, we began getting tantalizing glimpses of the Greater Himalayas. A pyramidical peak reminiscent of *Lost Horizon* was visible, its thick mantle of snow glistening in the sunlight against the clear blue sky. Incidentally, our assumption that the blue sky is endless turned out to be fallacious, one of the many fondly held beliefs that fell like ninepins with the rapid growth of scientific knowledge. As Lewis Thomas points out in *The Lives of a Cell*, the blue sky that we see is really only a delicate and fragile membrane that covers our planet and makes life possible. Beyond this there is the other sky, black and menacing, which was first seen by man when he ventured out of the gravitational pull of earth and made the first tentative probe into the vastness of outer space.

A few kilometres further up and one reached Nand Prayag, the confluence of the Mandakani and the Alaknanda, and then Pipalkoti. As one passed this tiny settlement, the great Himalayan range finally flashes into view, the 'Devatamat Himalaya' of Kalidasa, the most impressive natural object on our planet. This great range has nurtured untold generations of mankind since the dawn of history, and our own civilization owes its very existence to the power and wisdom that emanated from this great range of mountains. It has always seemed to me the height of human arrogance to talk of 'conquering' these great mountains just because a few adventurous people are able to crawl up to their peaks. I have no desire to denigrate the very real achievements of mountaineering, but I do feel that the terminology of conquest in these surroundings is totally inappropriate. Rather, the Vedic approach of awe and inspiration in the presence of these great symbols is more in keeping with our cultural ethos.

In the afternoon we reached Joshi Math where we stopped

at a tiny restaurant grandly named the Neelakantha Motel for a hurried lunch. A vehicle belonging to the Nanda Devi Expedition was parked outside, and some members of the support organization were in the restaurant. We also came across a group of Marwari businessmen from Calcutta who were making the pilgrimage along with us, and whose invitation to dinner at Badrinath we accepted somewhat impulsively. We left Joshi Math at about five. From there to Badrinath the traffic was only one way, although the road was as good as the earlier portions. The entire trip was unexpectedly warm, but we were grateful for the fine weather because the roads were in good condition. Beggars, including sadhus and local children, lined almost the entire length of the road which rose steadily to Badrinath, which is situated at an altitude of 10,300 feet above sea-level.

As we neared our destination there were some striking views of sheer rock and snow-covered peaks, and we finally reached Badrinath in the evening just before dark. The entire settlement is on an elevated plateau with snow mountains in the close background, the colourfully painted entrance to the shrine stands out from some distance. We were received by representatives of the temple authorities and taken to our rooms close to the shrine itself. The row of beggars continued literally up to the doorway of the shrine. The evening arati took place at 8 pm and we paid our first visit to the temple entering it through an entrance that was very Nepali in design and went up to the courtyard outside the sanctum sanctorum.

The arati and worship is performed by Namboodari

Brahmans from Kerala and this brings to mind the remarkable achievement of Adi Shankaracharya who, in a lifespan of only thirty-two years, virtually single-handedly revived Hinduism, wrote masterly commentaries upon all its major texts, and re-established the four great pilgrimage centres in the four corners of India. Surely if there is one historical person who should be considered the pioneer of national integration it was Adi Shankaracharya, and his remarkable fusion of intellectual and devotional power is almost unique in the history of religion.

After the arati we went around the temple and came across the famous Veena player Swami Parvatikar who was playing in the courtyard on an instrument invented by him which combines the Dattareya Veena and the Swarmandala. Swamiji is a musician of national fame, but he lives as a recluse in Badrinath for six months of the year. Fortunately, we had some more music before dinner because the Marwaris who had invited us were accompanied by Shrimati Kalyani, a well-known sitar player from Calcutta, At my request she gave a sensitive rendering of raga Bhupali, to my mind the most evocative of all the great ragas in the broad galaxy of Indian music.

By eight in the morning, we were in the temple again where a special puja was performed on our behalf and for some of the other pilgrims. The Garhwali pandits who chanted from texts in the courtyard were not outstanding, I have known better ones from that area, but the Namboodari inside the temple was excellent. Sanskrit has a strange evocative power, impressive not simply because of its meaning but for its rich cadence which speaks to the deeper layers of the human personality. The puja consisted of the entire ritual of bathing and anointing the black stone image to the accompaniment of chanting, while one of the temple functionaries related the legends connected with the temple culminating in its re-establishment by Shankara in the 14th century. All offerings were duly noted and receipts given, which itself is a welcome improvement as far as north Indian temples go. How I wish something could also be done about the beggars. Perhaps they could all be accommodated in a separate enclave and a certain percentage of the offering specifically earmarked for their maintenance. After the puja we returned to our rooms where two Pandas battled with each other to prove that they had the exclusive right to our patronage. My wife finally decided, virtually in self-defence, to pay both of them equally.

We left Badrinath at noon and returned to Joshi Math where we had coffee with a local Army Unit. I have had occasion to visit hundreds of units of the Indian Army in various parts of the country, and I never fail to be impressed by the quiet efficiency with which they adjust themselves to their surroundings. Thereafter we visited some beautiful temples in Joshi Math, a Krishna temple with some statues of outstanding artistic merit including those of Krishna, Balarama, an eight-armed Ganesha, and a Shiva-Parvati. Unfortunately, the entire temple was badly neglected and in an advanced stage of disrepair, and the famous Narasimha temple nearby was only in a slightly better condition.

By now the weather had begun to deteriorate, and soon

after we left Joshi Math the rain began to fall. For the next four hours we drove through heavy rain and hail, the mountains were barely visible and the whole scene transformed beyond recognition. It is always rather tricky driving on mountain roads during heavy rain, and we were glad when we finally passed the storm and reached Nand Prayag for a brief halt. We then continued our long drive back to Srinagar for the night, where the invisible flautist was still plying his art with rare devotion.

I had a good night at Srinagar, waking to an indefinable feeling that some problem had been solved, not at the intellectual but at some deeper level. For anyone who is on the spiritual path, dreams can provide an invaluable key to one's inner situation, and if properly interpreted can give important guidance. Indeed, it is now widely recognized that the human personality has many dimensions, of which the waking state of consciousness is only one. Dreams link us in some strange way not only with what Western psychotherapists would call the sub-conscious and the unconscious, but with the super and supraconscious levels of which yoga—the most profound enquiry into the mystery of the human personality ever attempted—speaks so clearly. A perceptive and sensitive awareness of our dreamlife can, therefore, be a most valuable and rewarding exercise.

On the return journey we stopped at Dev Prayag, the major confluence in this region where the Alakananda and the Bhagirathi rivers join to form the Ganga. Indeed, strictly speaking, the Ganga starts only from Dev Prayag downwards, and therefore this is a particularly holy spot. According to legend Sri Rama worshipped here for many years to expiate the sin incurred by his killing of the great Brahmin king of Lanka, and we were told that the large temple at Dev Prayag stands at the very place where Rama did his penance. We walked to this temple across what is known as the Rama Jhoola, a smaller version of the Lakshman Jhoola at Rishikesh. The black stone statue of Sri Rama is about 8 feet tall and would have been most impressive if properly decorated. Unfortunately, many of our deities in north India are so bundled up with coverings and cloth of various descriptions that they end up looking totally shapeless.

Descending once more to the plains we stopped again at Haridwar and had a marvellous bath in the Ganga, letting its cool current flow over us washing away not only the dust of the journey but all the cares and worries of the world. How truly had Jawaharlal Nehru said that the Ganga is the par excellence river of India. It is a comforting thought that when our life's journey finally ends our ashes will mingle in this great river which flows onwards in its eternal journey towards the sea. It is said that one can never step into the same river twice, because each time the river has changed. It is equally true that although apparently the same, our own personalities undergo constant modifications, and the person who returns from a pilgrimage is in some subtle way different from the one who sets out upon it.

BALI
(Late 1970s)

Imagine a small, mountainous island covered with coconut trees, palms, and lush rice fields, these terraced fields divided every few miles by deep gorges made by rapid streams running down to the sea, the villages made of thatched roofs and surrounded by small shrines. Then imagine a handsome race of people who could be straight out of the Kathmandu valley, with the same type of features and beautifully proportioned, smooth physiques. Imagine, finally, that these people are Hindus, and worship at beautifully carved, multi-tiered temples, which are like the Nepali temples at Patan and Bhatgaon. This is Bali, the enchanted island which Jawaharlal Nehru once described as 'the morning of the world'.

The Republic of Indonesia consists of over 17,000 islands. One of these is Bali, one of the twenty-seven provinces of Indonesia, with an area of just over 2000 square miles and a population of 23 lakhs, making it the country's second most densely populated island. The Indonesian islands, especially

Java, came under Indian influence as far back as AD 100. By AD 400 the first Hindu kingdoms on West Java and Borneo had risen to power, and their power increased to their zenith with the Shrivijaya and Mataram Kingdoms. Bali was part of the great Hindu kingdoms based in Java known as the Majapahit Kingdoms. These flourished for many centuries until the successive Muslim invasions ultimately succeeded in overthrowing them. With the fall of Majapahit, the Raja moved to Bali taking with him the entire court, including priests and artists; literally transplanting a whole culture to the island where it continues to flourish to this day. Ninety-five per cent of the inhabitants of Bali follow 'Hindu *Dharma*'. According to tradition, Hinduism was brought to Bali by four great Maharishis—Agastya and Markandeya from India, and Kuturaan and Dwijendra from Java.

Our Garuda Indonesian Airways plane landed at the Denpasar airport late in the evening. Looking out of the window as the plane descended, I could swear that we were landing somewhere in Kerala, and this impression deepened during the 15-km drive from the airport to the superb Oberoi Bali Beach Hotel during which we drove by thousands of coconut trees and rice fields. Hundreds of cloth scarecrows fluttered in the ripening fields to keep the birds away, and several huge paper kites were flying against the blue sky. These kites were in the shape of fish and dragons, and gave the curious feeling that we were in a strange land at the bottom of the sea looking at the fish swimming above us.

The Governor of Bali, a scholar named Dr. Ida Bagus

Mantra, had just completed a translation of the Bhagavad Gita into Balinese. As I drove to call on him at his residence that evening, I noticed a huge, beautifully sculptured statue of a four-headed Shiva standing on a lotus in one of the city circles, symbolising the way in which the Balinese have integrated iconographic symbols of Brahma, Vishnu, and Shiva into a harmonious unity, and over the centuries developed a graceful and unique pattern of Hinduism.

The next day we set out to visit the holiest shrine of Bali known as the Mother Temple at Besakih, situated on the slopes of the 3000-metre volcanic mountain Mount Agung (Agni). The whole of Indonesia consists of a chain of volcanic mountains that erupt from time to time, and in fact while we were there two volcanos were in a state of eruption over a 1000 miles away from Bali. When I heard the name Besakih I assumed that it was because of the Hindu month of Vaishakha, but it turned out to be based on Vasuki, the great serpent of Hindu mythology of which Krishna makes mention in the tenth chapter of the Gita when he says *Sarpanam asmi Vasuki*—Among the serpents I am Vasuki. It is curious that the only place in India I know where Vasuki is worshipped is the ancient principality of Bhadarwah in the Jammu region.

There is one major difference between the Bali temples and those in India. In Bali no images are worshipped, as they believe in worshipping the *achintya* (beyond thought) or *avyakta* (beyond form) aspect of the divine. The temple gates and the shrines themselves have beautifully sculptured figures of *dwarapalas*, but the actual worship is done to three niches representing Brahma, Vishnu, and Shiva. The Besakih complex is a series of temples built on terraces rising gently up the slopes of the volcano. On the highest terrace there is a large rectangular courtyard measuring at least 200 x 50 metres, and on this are the multitiered shrines so strikingly similar to Nepali architecture.

By a happy chance we arrived at the main shrine when a puja was in progress. A whole village of about 350 people—men, women and children—had come up from a village near the beach 80 km away, the women wearing flowers in their hair. They all sat quietly in the courtyard while their village priest and his wife performed the puja. After chanting mantras and throwing flowers from time to time towards the shrine, the priest rang a bell five times and each person responded with folded hands above their heads. Then there was the ritual *Abhishekha*, sprinkling of water on the devotees, the *Charanamrita*, sipping the sacred water, and then the whole party descended the slopes for the long journey home. The Besakih temple has its main pilgrimage during the Vaishakha Purnima when over a million people from all over Bali and other parts of Indonesia come to worship there. In 1943 there was a serious volcanic eruption which killed 25,000 people, but miraculously the temple escaped untouched except for some entrance portals that were later repaired.

Each village has its own priest, the Pedanda, while each shrine has its temple priest known as the Pamanku. While the village priest is always a Brahmin—man or woman—the temple priests can be of any of the four castes. Temples are dedicated to various deities of the Hindu pantheon, but always without images in the main shrine.

Most villages have small shrines in the fields dedicated to the Rice Goddess, Brahma-Vishnu temples in the main village, and Shiva-Durga temples near the cremation grounds. The temples are known in Balinese as Puras, and they are often constructed near sacred banyan trees, while in Java the Hindu temple is known as Chandi.

Bali was divided between nine kings (Rajas), of whom one was the Maharaja known as the Dewi Agung Klung Kung. Our guide on the drive was a bright young officer from the Bali protocol department named Paramartha Kesuma, and during our conversation I realized how very close Balinese is to Sanskrit, apparently as close as many of the Indian languages themselves. Their greeting is *Aum Swastiastu*, the ocean is *Sagara*; the volcano is *Agun Parvata*; the flowers are *Pushpa*; food *Bhojana*; the bull *nandaka* ; and the cow *nandini*; while their days of the week are also based on Sanskrit. An interesting point, which highlights the deep cultural links with India, is to be found in the Balinese words for the directions. While north is 'uttara', east 'purva' and south 'dakshina', the word for west is 'barata'. India, of course, is to the west of Bali!

There is some controversy regarding the origin of the word 'Bali' itself. Perhaps it is based on the word 'Bali', sacrifice, or more likely, associated with one of the Hindu kings of ancient mythology. It seems to me that there could well be a link with the Raja Bali of the Puranas who was banished by Vishnu in his Vamana Avatara to live in the underworld. Java and Bali are indeed the 'underworld' geographically vis a vis India, located as they are well south of the Equator. The names in Bali and indeed even in other parts of Indonesia that are Muslim, are largely Sanskrit based. Thus, the girls have names like Pushpawati, Chandrawati, Kusumawati, and Padmawati, while the boys like Mahendra, Rajendra, and Yoga. The shops in Bali have evocative names which could advantageously be adopted in Connaught Circus—Raj Yamuno, Eka Linga, Surya Kenchana, Devi Sitha, Dharma Sutra, etc.

On our return we visited some of the workshops which produced superb Balinese art objects. By far the most impressive are the wood carvings done either in black ebony or blond wood. Using to full advantage the contours of the wood, the Balinese artists produced the most superb elongated figures of Hindu mythological figures, birds, and animals. The same grace is found in the Balinese dance, which is a charming amalgam of Bharatnatyam, Kathakali, and Odissi movements. The *Ramayana*, of course, is the most popular theme, but many episodes are taken from the *Mahabharata*. The *Ramayana* must surely be one of the most influential epics ever written. The impact of the immortal story of Sri Rama and Devi Sita continues to reverberate throughout Southeast Asia, and in Bali it was visible in all rich glory. The Pandavas also figure prominently in Balinese art. An interesting angle pointed out by our Muslim guide later in Java was that the five Pandavas are believed to represent the five sheaths of man—Nakula the physical; Sahadeva the etheric, Arjuna the desire, Bhima the thought, and Yudhishthira the wisdom. While in India

Bhima is known for his feats of strength, in Indonesia a whole cult of Bhima developed in the 13th century as representing the intellectual power of man. Another twist is that while in India Shakuni is considered to be the evil genius behind the Kauravas, in Indonesia it is Dronacharya who is the villain. Perhaps this symbolised the Brahmin-Kshatriya rivalry in the Javan kingdoms, which were all founded and dominated by the Kshatriya dynasties.

It is interesting that though Indonesia is a predominantly Muslim state, there is full freedom of religion for other faiths including Hinduism. Indeed, in Bali there is a planned effort to develop the Hindu cultural heritage. This includes the setting up recently of the Institute of Hindu Dharma with 1600 students divided into three faculties—Religion and Culture, Religion and Society, Religion and Education. It offers a five-year programme from the under-graduate to the post-graduate level, and apart from Balinese it teaches Bahasa Indonesia and Sanskrit. It is financed by fees and a government subsidy, and offers an excellent avenue for developing cultural relations between India and Indonesia.

Bali has some of the most beautiful beaches in the world and its architecture has also retained a rare integrity. Apart from one high-rise hotel, which the authorities now regret, the government ensures that all new buildings harmonise with traditional Balinese architecture. The new and most impressive cultural complex with an arts centre, a music school and a huge amphitheatre that can seat 5000 people for the *Ramayana* festival is built in what may be called the Hindu style of architecture, and would require a visit by some of our modern architects who look down on traditional motifs in India.

While Bali is fascinating, especially for visitors from India interested in our cultural heritage, the real glory of Hindu architecture lies in Java, the cultural heart of the great Indonesian archipelago. It is here that the great Hindu empires rose and flourished in the 8th and 9th centuries, when the Emperors Sailendra and Sanjaya founded their kingdoms, and where two of the world's greatest monuments still stand—Borobodur and Prambanan, one, the greatest Buddhist monument in the world, and the other, the greatest Hindu temple in Southeast Asia after Angkor. Both of these were built within thirty years of each other, Borobodur in AD 824 and Prambanan in AD 856 and both lie close to the old capital of Yogjakarta, an hour's flight from Bali.

The volcanic nature of the Indonesian archipelago is clearly revealed from the air, from which one can see dozens of volcanic mountains with their characteristic cone shaped slopes topped by a crater. On landing at Yogjakarta, one sees three great volcanic peaks, each over 3000 metres high, which dominate central Java, the highest being known as the Mahameru, the sacred peak of the Hindus.

Borobodur (Bhadra Vihara), about an hour's drive from the town, is a breathtaking monument. Conceived and built as a huge mandala, it contains no fewer than 368 statues of the Buddha, each enclosed in a bell-shaped stupa, which rise tier upon circular tier to a huge stupa in the centre of the monument. Climbing several flights of steep steps, one comes finally to the highest terrace which is fanned by a cool breeze and presents a lovely view of Mahameru. The sheer size and unique design of the monument, with scenes from the *Mahabharata* and *Ramayana* engraved on its sides, makes it of world importance. UNESCO has in fact made substantial grants to supplement the efforts of the Indonesian government for reconstruction and renovation of Borobodur, which has frequently been damaged by the recurrent earthquakes in the area.

The Prambanan (Param Brahman) temple complex is in some ways even more impressive. It is also built in the form of a yantra and consists of a great central temple dedicated to Lord Shiva, auxiliary temples to Vishnu and Brahma, five smaller temples and dozens of shrines all in one great courtyard. The main temple is extremely impressive, and rivals the great Brihadishwara Temple in Thanjavur. The temple is used for religious worship once every nine years. Its main shrine opening to the east is dedicated to Shiva, while to the south is Agastya, to the west Ganesha, and to the north Durga. The temple was seriously damaged by an earthquake, but it is most gratifying to see that the Indonesian government has undertaken a massive reconstruction programme to rebuild the entire complex.

It is strange that this tremendous cultural efflorescence of Hinduism in Southeast Asia is barely known back in India. Who were the great kings, and priests and artisans who ventured forth thousands of miles from the mother country over fifteen centuries ago? How did they cross the stormy oceans, what sort of people did they find in these islands, how did they establish their great kingdoms, and build their fabulous temples? What unsung epics of valour and wisdom must there be for these exploits before which the much-lionized voyage of Columbus to America pales? Is it not time at last that this aspect of Indian history should be rediscovered?

Meanwhile, the island of Bali lying like a lush jewel just off the mainland of Java, remains a living symbol of the unconquerable vitality of Hinduism.

PART FOUR

Selections from Hindu Texts and Seers

(All translations in this section are by Eknath Easwaran, A.C. Bose and the author.)

RIG VEDA

Lead me from unreality to reality
Lead me from darkness to light
Lead me from death to immortality.

***

Hymn of Creation

In the beginning
There was neither existence nor non-existence,
Neither sky nor heaven beyond…

That One breathed, without breath, by its own power,
Nothing else was there…

The first born was the Creative Will,
The primordial seed of the mind.
The sages, searching for the truth within their own hearts,
Realised the eternal bond between the seen and unseen.

This bond was an endless line stretched across the heavens.
What was above?
What was below?
Primal seeds were sprouting, mighty forces moving,
Pulsation below, pure energy above.

Who here knows? Who can say for sure
When it began and from where it came—this creation?
The gods came afterwards,
So who really knows

From where this creation came,
Whether He formed it or not.
He who watches everything from the highest heaven,
Only He knows—or perhaps even He does not know!

***

The Path of Unity

Meet together, speak together,
 let your minds be of one accord,
 as the Devas of old, being of one mind,
 accepted their share of sacrifice.

May your counsel be common, your
 assembly common, common the
 mind, and the thoughts of these united.

A common purpose do I lay before you,
 and worship with your common oblation.

Let your aims be common,
and your hearts of one accord, and all
of you be of one mind,
so you may live well together.'

***

Surya

Up rises the beautiful orb
on the near margin of the sky,
as the divine white-coloured steed
bears it fast, making it visible to all

The Sun, shining on all, crest by crest,
the lord of what moves and what stands still,
the seven-sister bays bear in the chariot
for the well-being of the world.

That eye, divinely placed, rising bright,
may we see for a hundred autumns.
And may we live for a hundred autumns.

ATHARVA VEDA

Who knows Him, knows himself,
and is not afraid to die.

***

Hymn to the Earth

Truth, Eternal, Order that is great and stern,
Consecration, Austerity, Prayer and Ritual—these uphold the Earth.
May she, Queen of what has been and will be, make a wide world for us.

Earth which has many heights, and slopes and the unconfined
plain that bind men together,
Earth that bears plants of various healing powers,
may she spread wide for us and thrive.

Earth, in which lie the sea, the river and other waters,
in which food and cornfields have come to be,
in which live all that breathes and that moves,
may she confer on us the finest of her yield.

Mistress of four quarters, in whom food and cornfields have come to be,
who bears in many forms the breathing and moving life,
may she give us cattle and crops.

Earth, in which men of old before us performed their various work,
where Devas overwhelmed the Asuras, Earth, the home of kine, horses, birds,
may she give us magnificence and lustre.

All-sustaining, treasure-bearing, firm staying-place,
gold-breasted, home of all moving life,
Earth bears the sacred universal fire.
May Indra and Rishava give us wealth.

Earth, whom unsleeping Devas protect forever without erring,
may she pour on us delicious sweets, and endow us with lustre.

Earth, which at first was in the water of the ocean,
and which sages sought with wondrous powers,
Earth whose heart was in Eternal Heaven, wrapped in Truth, immortal,
may she give us lustre and strength in a most exalted State.

Earth, in which the waters, common to all, moving on all sides, flow
unfailing, day and night,
may she pour on us milk in many streams, and endow us with lustre.

Earth, in which the Asvins measured out and Vishnu strode,
which Indra, Lord of might, made free from foes for himself,
may she pour out milk for me—a mother to her son.

Pleasant be thy hills, O Earth, thy snow-clad mountains and thy woods!
On Earth—brown, black, ruddy and multi-coloured—the firm
Earth protected by Indra,
on this Earth I stand, unvanquished, unslain, unhurt.

Set me, O Earth, amidst what is thy centre and thy navel,
and vitalising forces that emanated from thy body.
Purify us from all sides.
Earth is my mother, her son am I; and Parjanya my father:
may he fill us with plenty.

Earth, on which they build up the altar,
and various workers spin the web of Yajna,
on which are fixed the tall, bright poles before the invocation;
may she, prospering, make us prosper.

The man, O Earth, who hates us, is hostile to us,
who threatens us by his thoughts and his weapons,
overwhelm him, Earth, as thou hast done before.

Born of thee, on thee move mortal creatures;
thou bearest them—the biped and the quadruped.
Thine, O Earth, are the five races of men to whom, mortals,
the sun as he rises spreads, with his rays, the light immortal.

In concert may all creatures pour out blessing!
Endow me, Earth, that honied speech.

Mother of all plants, firm Earth upheld by Eternal Law,
may she be ever beneficent and gracious to us as we tread on her.
A vast abode art thou, and mighty,
and mighty is thy speed, thy moving and thy shaking;
and mighty Indra protects thee unerring.
May thou, O Earth, make us shine forth with the brightness of gold.
Let no one hate me.

There lies the fire within the earth,
and in plants, and waters carry it;
the fire is in stone.
There is a fire deep within men,
a fire in the kine,
and a fire in horses:

The same fire that burns in the heavens;
the mid-air belongs to this Fire Divine.
Men kindle this fire that bears the Oblation
and loves the melted butter.

May Earth, clad in her fiery mantle, dark-kneed,
make me a flame; may she sharpen me bright.

Earth on which they offer yajna and oblation to Devas with many decorations,
on which mortal men live by food and drink:
may she give us breath and life,
may she make us long-lived.

The fragrance that rises from thee, O Earth,
that plants and waters carry, and is shared by Gandharvas, by Apsarases,
make me sweet with that,
May no one hate me.

Thy fragrance that is in men and women,
and the majesty and lustre in males,
in the hero and the steed,
in the wild beast and in the elephant,
and the radiance that is in the maiden,
unite us with these, O Earth!
May no one hate me.

Rock, soil, stone, and dust,
Earth is held together and bound firm.
To her my obeisance, to gold-breasted Earth.
We invoke all-supporting Earth
on which trees, lords of forests, stand ever firm.

Rising or sitting, standing, or walking,
May we, either with our right foot or our left,
never totter on the earth.

I call to Earth, the purifier, the patient Earth,
growing strong through spiritual might.
May we recline on thee, O Earth,
who bearest power, plenty, our share of food and molten butter.

Pure may the waters flow for our bodies' cleansing.
To those who trespass against us
we offer an unpleasant welcome.
I cleanse myself, O Earth, with that which purifies.

May those that are thy eastern regions, and the northern, Earth,
and the southern and the western,
be pleasant for me to tread upon.
May I not stumble while I live in the world.

Do not push me from the west or from the east,
or from the north or the south.
Be gracious to us, O Earth.
Let not those find us who waylay people on the road.
Take deadly weapons far away from us.

So long as I look on thee from around, O Earth, with the sun as friend,
So long, as year follows year, may not my vision fail.

When, lying down, O Earth,
I turn on my right side and on my left,
or when we lie straight on our ribs against thee behind us,
be thou not unkind to us then, O Earth,
thou who layest all to sleep.

Whatever I dig from thee, Earth,
may that have quick growth again.
O purifier, may we not injure thy vitals or thy heart.

May thy summer, Earth, and thy rains,
thy autumn, thy dewy months, thy winter and thy spring,
may these thy seasons, Earth, that make the year,
and day and night, pour their abundance on us.

She, purifier, who kept away from the Serpent,
and carried the fires within her waters,
she, Earth, having opted for Indra and not Vritra,
drove away the God-hating Dasyus,
and held on to Sakra, the strong and mighty.

Earth, on which the sacred seat and shed are built, and the pole is raised;
on which Brahmanas, versed in Yajus, worship in Rig and Sama hymns,
and priests are busy so that Indra may drink the Soma juice;
On which, of old, world-building Rishis chanted the sacred words,
and the Seven Sages prayed in session with sacrifice and austerity;

May that Earth grant us the wealth that we desire.
May Bhaga give the task, and Indra come to lead the way.

Earth, on which men sing and dance while uttering various words,
where people meet in battle, the war-cry rises, the drum sounds,
may she drive away our enemies; may Earth make me free from foes.

Earth on which grow food-grains—rice and barley,
on which live the five races of men;
our homage be to her, Parjanya's Consort, who mellows with the rain.

Earth, in which are cities, the work of Devas,
and fields where men are variously employed;
Earth that bears all things in her womb,
may the Lord of Life make her graceful for us from every side.

May Earth with people who speak various tongues,
and those who have various religious rites according to their places of abode,
pour for me treasure in a thousand streams, like a constant cow that never fails.

The snake, and the scorpion with the sharp sting,
that, overpowered by the cold season, lie bewildered in the caves,
the worm and each thing that comes to life, O Earth, and
moves about with the coming of rains,
may these, creeping, never creep near us.

Bless us with what is beneficent.

Thy many pathways for men to travel on,
the roads for chariots, and for wagons to pass through,
on which walk together both good and evil men,
may we be master of those, and drive out thief and foe.

Earth bearing the weighty also bears the foolish,
and endures the death of both the good and the bad,

and, being of one accord with the boar,
she lets loose the swine to roam wildly about.

Those thy forest animals, and wild beasts of the woods—
lions, tigers, man-eaters that prowl about,
and the hyena, the wolf, the bear with its evil ways, and Rakshas,
drive these out, O Earth, from here, away from us.
And, Earth, drive away from us
Gandharvas, Apsarasas, Arayas, Kimidins, Pisachas, and all Rakshasas.

Earth, to which the winged bipeds fly together—
swans, eagles, and other birds of various kinds,
on which the wind blows strong, raising the dust, bending trees,
and flame follows the blast forward and backward;

Earth, in which Night and Day—the black and the bright in union—are settled,
which is covered and canopied over by rain—
may she establish us with bliss in every dear home.

Heaven, Earth, and Mid-air have given me this wide space,
And Agni, Surya, Apas, and All-Gods
have together endowed me with the intellect.

I am victorious,
I am called the most exalted on the earth,
a conqueror everywhere,
a conqueror over everything,
I am a victor on every side.

When, O Goddess, proceeding forward,
and extolled by Devas, thou hadst spread thy renown,
then a great glory entered into thee,
and thou madest for thyself the four quarters.

In villages, in the forest, and in the assemblies on the earth,
in congregations and in councils,
we shall speak of thee in lovely terms.

As a horse scatters dust, so did Earth, since she was born,
scatter the people who dwelt on the land,
and she joyously sped on—the world's protectress,
supporter of forests, trees, and plants.

What I speak, I speak with sweetness;
what I look at endears itself to me;
and I am fiery and impetuous:
others who fly at me with wrath I smite down.

Peaceful, sweet-smelling, gracious, filled with milk,
and bearing nectar in her breast,
may Earth give with the milk her blessings to me.

With oblation, Visvakarman sought her
who had entered the light in the mid-air's ocean,
And the delicious vessel hidden in Mystery
became manifest for the nurture of those who found in her their Mother.

Thou art the vessel, the Mother of the people, the fulfiller of wishes, far-extending.

Whatever is wanting in thee is filled by Prajapati, firstborn of Eternal Order.

May those born of thee, O Earth,
be, for our welfare, free from sickness and waste.
Wakeful through a long life, we shall become bearers of tribute to thee.

Earth, my Mother! set me securely with bliss, in full accord with Heaven,
Wise One, uphold me in grace and splendour.

THE ISHA UPANISHAD

All this is full. All that is full.
From fullness, fullness comes.
When fullness is taken of fullness,
Fullness still remains.

The Lord is enshrined in the hearts of all.
The Lord is the supreme Reality.
Rejoice in him through renunciation.
Covet nothing. All belongs to the Lord,
Thus working may you live a hundred years.

Thus alone will you work in real freedom.

Those who deny the Self are born again
Blind to the Self, enveloped in darkness,
Utterly devoid of love for the Lord.
The Self is one. Ever still, the Self is
Swifter than thought, swifter that the senses.
Though motionless, he outruns all pursuit.
Without the Self, never could life exist.

The Self seems to move, but is ever still.
He seems far away, but is ever near.
He is within all, and he transcends all.

Those who see all creatures in themselves
And themselves in all creatures know no fear.

Those who see all creatures in themselves
How can the multiplicity of life,
Delude the one who sees its unity?

The Self is everywhere. Bright is the Self,
Indivisible, untouched by sin, wise,
Immanent and transcendent. He it is
Who holds the cosmos together.

In dark night live those for whom
The world without alone is real; in night
Darker still, for whom the world within
Alone is real. The first leads to a life
Of action, the second to a life of meditation.

But those who combine action with Meditation,
Cross the sea of death through action
And enter into immortality,
Through the practice of meditation
So have we heard from the wise.

In dark night live those for whom the Lord
Is transcendent only; in night darker still,
For whom he is immanent only.

But those for whom he is transcendent
And immanent, cross the sea of death
With the immanent and enter into
Immortality with the transcendent.
So have we heard from the wise.

The face of truth is hidden by your orb
Of gold, O sun. May you remove your orb,
So that I, who adore the true, may see.

The glory of truth, O nourishing sun,
Solitary traveller, controller,
Source of life for all creatures, spread your light,

And subdue your dazzling splendour
So that I may see your blessed Self.
Even that very Self am I!

May my life merge in the Immortal
When my body is reduced to ashes.
O mind, meditate on the eternal Brahman.

Remember the deeds of the past.
Remember, O mind, remember.

O god of fire, lead us by the good path
To eternal joy. You know all our deeds.
Deliver us from evil, we who bow
And pray again and again.

SHVETASHVATARA UPANISHAD

Though the Indefinite One is without colour,
He colours the entire universe;
Though immortal, He is born, lives, and dies.

That One is all that was, is, and will be;
Yet He is always the same,
He is the Supreme, Unchanging Absolute.

He becomes the fire, the sun,
The wind, the moon;
He becomes the starry heavens,
The vast waters, giving life to all.

He becomes the woman, the man,
The youth and the maiden too;
He becomes the old person
Tottering on his staff;
Looking in every direction.
He becomes the blue butterfly,
The green parrot with red eyes;

he becomes lightning, the seasons,
The endless seas.

Without birth or death,
Beyond all time and space,
He is the One from whom
Every world is born.

The Lord of all,
The knower of all,
The beginning and end of all—
That Self dwells in every human heart.

It is the final resting place of all activity,
peaceful and unchanging,
the ultimate good,
one without a second,
It is the Supreme Self.
It, above all else, should be known.

TAITTIRIYA UPANISHAD

When the Master has declared Veda, then he gives the commandments to his disciple.

Speak truth, walk in the way of thy duty, neglect not the study of Veda. When thou hast brought to the Master the wealth that he desires, thou shalt not cut short the long thread of thy race. Thou shalt not be negligent of thy duty, thou shalt not be negligent of welfare; and thy thriving; thou shalt not be negligent of the study and teaching of Veda.

Thou shalt not be negligent of thy works unto the Gods or thy works unto the Fathers. Let thy father be unto thee as thy God and thy mother as thy Goddess whom thou adorest. Serve the Master as a God and as a God the stranger within thy dwelling. The works that are without blame before the people, thou shalt do these with diligence and no others. The deeds we practise these as a religion and no others.

Whosoever are better and nobler than we among the Brahmins, thou shalt refresh with a seat to honour them. Thou shalt give with faith and reverence; without faith thou shalt not give. Thou shalt give with shame, thou shalt give with fear; thou shalt give with fellow-feeling.

BRIHADARANYAKA UPANISHAD

JANAKA:
'When the sun sets, Yajnavalkya, and the moon sets, and the fire goes out and no one speaks, what is the light of man?'

YAJNAVALKYA:
'The Self indeed is the light of man, your majesty, for by that we sit, work, go out, and come back.'

JANAKA:
'Who is that Self?'

YAJNAVALKYA:
'The Self, pure awareness, shines as the light within the heart, surrounded by the senses. Only seeming to think, seeming to move, the Self neither sleeps nor wakes nor dreams. When the Self takes on a body, he seems to assume the body's frailties and limitations; but when he sheds the body at the time of death, the Self leaves all these behind.

'The human being has two states of consciousness: one in this world, the other in the next. But there is a third state between them, not unlike the world of dreams, in which we are aware of both worlds, with their sorrows and joys. When a person dies, it is only the physical body that dies; that person lives on in a nonphysical body, which carries the impression of his past life. It is these impressions that determine his next life. In this intermediate state he makes and dissolves impressions by the light of the Self.

'In that third state of consciousness there are no chariots, no horses drawing them on roads on which to travel, but he makes up his own chariots, horses, and roads. In that state there are no joys or pleasures, but he makes up his own joys and pleasures. In that state there are no lotus ponds, no lakes, no rivers, but he makes up his own lotus ponds, lakes, and rivers. It is he who makes up all these from the impressions of his past or waking life.

'It is said of these states of consciousness that in the dreaming state, when one is sleeping, the shining Self, who never dreams, who is ever awake, watches by his own light the dreams woven out of past deeds and present desires. In the dreaming state, when one is sleeping, the shining Self keeps the body alive with the vital force of *prana*, and wanders wherever he wills. In the dreaming state, when one is sleeping, the shining Self assumes many forms, eats with friends, indulges in sex, sees fearsome spectacles.

'But he is not affected by anything because he is detached and free; and after wandering here and there in the state of dreaming, enjoying pleasures and seeing good and evil, he returns to the state from which he began.

'As a great fish swims between the banks of a river as

it likes, so does the shining Self move between the states of dreaming and waking.

'As an eagle, weary after soaring in the sky, folds its wings and flies down to rest in its nest, so does the shining Self enter the state of dreamless sleep, where one is freed from all desires.

'The Self is free from desire, free from evil, free from fear.

'As a man in the arms of his beloved is not aware of what is without and what is within, so a person in union with the Self is not aware of what is without and what is within, for in that unitive state all desires find their perfect fulfilment. There is no other desire that needs to be fulfilled, and one goes beyond sorrow.

'In that unitive state there is neither father nor mother, neither worlds, nor gods nor even scriptures. In that state there is neither thief nor slayer, neither low caste nor high, neither monk nor ascetic. The Self is beyond good and evil, beyond all the suffering of the human heart.

'In that unitive state one sees without seeing, for there is nothing separate from him; smells without smelling, for there is nothing separate from him; tastes without tasting, for there is nothing separate from him; speaks without speaking, for there is nothing separate from him; hears without hearing, for there is nothing separate from him; touches without touching, for there is nothing separate from him; thinks without thinking, for there is nothing separate from him; knows without knowing, for there is nothing separate from him.

'When there is separateness, one sees another, smells another, tastes another, speaks to another, hears another, touches another, thinks of another, knows another.

'But where there is unity, one without a second, that is the world of Brahman. This is the supreme goal of life, the supreme treasure, the supreme joy. Those who do not seek this supreme goal live on but a fraction of this joy.'

JANAKA:
'I give you another thousand cows! Please teach me more of the way to Self-realisation.'

YAJNAVALKYA:
'As a heavily laden cart creaks as it moves along, the body groans under its burden when a person is about to die. When the body grows weak through old age or illness, the Self separates himself, as a mango or fig or banyan fruit frees itself from the stalk, and returns the way he came to begin another life.

'Just as when a king is expected to visit a village, the mayor and all the other officials turn out to welcome him with food and drink, all creation awaits the person who sheds his body having realised Brahman. 'Here he comes!' they say. 'Here comes Brahman himself!' But the senses, while that man lies dying, gather around and mourn the Self departure, as courtiers mourn when their king is about to leave.

'When body and mind grow weak, the Self gathers in all the powers of life and descends with them into the heart. As *prana* leaves the eye, it ceases to see. 'He is becoming one,' say the wise; 'he does not see. He is becoming one; he can no longer see. He is becoming one; he no longer speaks, or tastes, or smells, or thinks, or knows. By the light of the heart the Self leaves the body by one of its gates; and when he leaves, *prana* follows, and with it all the vital powers of the body. He who is dying merges in consciousness, and thus consciousness accompanies him when he departs, along with the impression of all that he has done, experienced, and known.

'As a caterpillar, having come to the end of one blade of grass, draws itself together and reaches out for the next, so the Self, having come to the end of one life and dispelled all ignorance, gathers in his faculties and reaches out from the old body to a new.

'As a goldsmith fashions an old ornament into a new and more beautiful one, so the Self, having reached the end of the last life and dispelled all ignorance, makes for himself a new, more beautiful shape, like that of the devas or other celestial beings.

'The Self is indeed Brahman, but through ignorance people identify it with intellect, mind, senses, passions, and the elements of earth, water, air, space, and fire. This is why the Self is said to consist of this and that, and appears to be everything.

'As a person acts, so he becomes in life. Those who do good become good; those who do harm become bad. Good deeds make one pure; bad deeds make one impure. So we are said to be what our desire is. As our desire is, so is our will. As our will is, so are our acts. As we act, so we become.

'We live in accordance with our deep, driving desire. It is desire at the time of death that determines what our next life is to be. We will come back to earth to work out the satisfaction of that desire.

'But not those who are free from desire; they are free because all their desires have found fulfilment in the Self. They do not die like the others; but realising Brahman, they merge in Brahman. So, it is said:

When all the desires that surge in the heart
Are renounced, the mortal becomes immortal.

When all the knots that strangle the heart

Are loosened, the mortal becomes immortal,
Here in this very life.

'As the skin of a snake is sloughed onto an anthill, so does the mortal body fall; but the Self, freed from the body, merges in Brahman, infinite life, eternal light.'

JANAKA:
'I give you another thousand cows! Please teach me more of the way to Self-realisation.'

YAJNAVALKYA:
'Those who realise the Self enter into the peace that brings complete self-control and perfect patience. They see themselves in everyone and everyone in themselves. Evil cannot overcome them because they overcome all evil. Sin cannot consume them because they consume all sin. Free from evil, free from sin and doubt, they live in the kingdom of Brahman. Your majesty, this kingdom is yours!'

JANAKA:
'Venerable One, I offer myself and my kingdom in your service.'

MANDUKYA UNPANISHAD

AUM *[OM]* stands for the supreme Reality.
It is a symbol for what was, what is,
And what shall be. A U M represents also
What lies beyond past, present, and future.

Brahman is all, and the Self is Brahman.
This Self has four states of consciousness.

The first is called Vaishvanara, in which
One lives with all the senses turned outward,
Aware only of the external world.

Taijasa is the name of the second,
The dreaming state in which, with the senses

Turned inward, one enacts the impressions
Of past deeds and present desires.

The third state is called Prajna, of deep sleep,
In which one neither dreams nor desires.
There is no mind in Prajna, there is no

Separateness; but the sleeper is not
Conscious of this. Let him become conscious
In Prajna and it will open the door
To the state of abiding joy.

Prajna, all-powerful and all-knowing,
Dwells in the hearts of all as the ruler.
Prajna is the source and end of all.

The fourth is the superconscious state called Turiya,
Neither inward nor outward,
Beyond the senses and the intellect,
In which there is none other than the Lord,

He is the supreme goal of life. He is
Infinite peace and love. Realise him!

Turiya is represented by AUM,
Thought indivisible, it has three sounds:
A stands for Vaishvanara;
Those who know this,
Through mastery of the senses, obtain
The fruit of their desires and attain greatness.

U stands for Taijasa;
Those who know this,
By mastering even their dreams, become
Established in wisdom. In their family
Everyone leads the spiritual life.

M stands for Prajna;
Those who know this,

By stilling the mind, find their true stature
And inspire everyone around to grow.

The mantra AUM stands for the supreme state
Of Turiya, without parts, beyond birth
And death, a symbol of everlasting joy.
Those who know AUM as the Self become the Self;

Truly they become the Self.

CHANDOGYA UPANISHAD

Twelfth Khanda

1 The father said: 'Fetch me from thence a fruit of the Nyagrodha tree.'
The son brought it, 'Here is one, sir.'
'Break it.'
'It is broken, sir.'
'These seeds are almost infinitesimal. Break one of them. What do you see there?'
'Nothing, sir. 'Not anything, sir.'

2 The father said: 'My son, that subtle essence which you do not perceive there, of that very essence this great Nyagrodha tree exists.
'Believe it, my son. That which is the subtle essence, in it all that exists has its self. It is the True. It is the Self, and thou, O Svetaketu, art it.'
'Please, sir, inform me still more,' said the son.
'Be it so, my child,' the father replied.

Thirteenth Khanda

1 Place this salt in water, and then wait on me in the morning.'
The son did as he was commanded.
The father said to him : 'Bring me the salt, which you placed in the water last night.'

The son having looked for it, found it not, for, of course, it was dissolved.

2 The father said : 'Taste it from the surface of the water. How is it?'
The son replied: 'It is salt.'
'Taste it from the middle. How is it?'
The son replied: 'It is salt.'
'Taste it from the bottom. How is it?'
The son replied: 'It is salt.'
The father said: 'Throw it away and then wait on me.'

Then the father said: 'As salt exists for ever, here also, in this body, for sooth, you do not perceive the True, my son; but there indeed it is.'

3 'That which is the subtle essence, in it all that exists has its self. It is the True. It is the Self, and thou, O Svetaketu, art it.'
'Please, sir, inform me still more,' said the son. 'Be it so, my child.' The father replied.

SRIMAD BHAGAVAD GITA

Divine Manifestations

LORD KRISHNA:
I am the source of everything,
and all worlds come out of Me;
knowing this, the wise ones honour me
in the cave of their hearts.

Dwelling within as pure consciousness,
I destroy the darkness born of ignorance
with the shining lamp of true knowledge.

O Arjuna! Of all creation
I am the beginning, middle, and end;
I am the supreme knowledge of the Self,
the eloquence of every orator.

I am Death, devourer of all,
and also the origin of all things yet to be;

among the feminine virtues
I am fame, fortune,
eloquence, wisdom, gratitude,
patience, and forgiveness.

O Arjuna, I am the primal seed
of all existence;
no being, moving or unmoving,
can exist without me.

All that exist,
all that is beautiful, radiant, and powerful,

is but a spark of my brilliant Light...

***

Vision of God's Form

If the light of a thousand suns
were to blaze in the sky at once,
such would hardly match the splendour
of that Great Being.

O Arjuna, only by the
unswerving love of a human heart,
can my supreme state be seen,
and known, and attained.

***

Purushottam Yoga

LORD KRISHNA:
They say there is an eternal pipal-tree
with roots on high and branches downward.

The verses of Scripture are its leaves.
Who understands this tree understands
the Scriptures.

It stretches its branches
Upward and downward.
The states of all things
Nurture the young shoots.
The young shoots are
The nourishment of our senses.
And below,
The roots go far
Into the world of men;
They are the sequences of actions.

This understanding
Of the tree's shape—
Its end and its beginning,
And its ground—
Is not open to
The ordinary world.
The roots of that pipal
Have spread far
With the strong axe

Of detachment
A man should cut
That tree.

Then he should search
For that place whence
Men who have found it
Do not return.
He should search for it
And reflect:
'I take refuge
In the very first Divine Being.
The whole world came,
The whole world stretched forth
From Him.'

Men without delusions
Go to that
Everlasting place.
They are humble,
Sincere people.
They have overcome
The damage
Done by attachments.
They are intent
Uninterruptedly
On that which is Real.
Desires have dwindled away.
From opposites as we know them—

Joy, grief—
They are set free.

Neither sun, moon, nor fire
lights up the place they reach,
From which no one returns.
That is my supreme abode.

Part of me has become the life of the world.

Everlasting, yet in the world of the living,
This part absorbs the senses and mind,
Whose home is in matter.
Whatever body the Lord takes on, or, upon death, leaves,
He grasps and holds those senses and mind
As the wind carries fragrances from place to place.

The Lord takes his stand upon
hearing, sight, touch, taste, smell,
And upon the mind.
He enjoys what mind and senses enjoy.

Deluded men cannot trace his course.
Only the eye of wisdom sees him
Clothed in the states of existence, going
forth, being in the body, or taking in experience.

Disciplined men can also make an effort
and see his presence in themselves.
Senseless men, far from perfection,
never see him, in spite of their efforts.

The splendour in sun, moon, and fire
illumines the entire world.
That splendour is mine.

I enter the earth, and I uphold
all creatures by my might.
I become Soma, the very sap of life,
and I nourish all plants.

I become the fire of life
and dwell in the bodies of the living.
Ignited by the breaths
I digest all the four sorts of food.

And in everyone's heart
I am present.
From me come
Knowledge of tradition,
Wisdom And reasoning.
I am the object
Of all the Scriptures.
I am the knower of the Scriptures.
I have established their purpose.

There are two spirits in the world,
one perishable, one imperishable.
All creatures together form the perishable,
the imperishable is that which is on high.

Other that these two is the highest being,
known as the supreme reality.

He, the eternal Lord, enters the threefold world—

of gods, men, and the realm between—and carries it.

I go beyond the perishable
and I transcend also the imperishable.
Therefore, the world and Scripture
celebrate me as the Highest Being.

Whatever man is free from all obsessions
thus knows me as the Highest Being,
Knows all. He loves and worships me
in all ways of worship and love.

I have imparted to you, man without
blame, the most secret teachings.
If a man sees their light, he will be enlightened,
and what he should do is done, son of Bharata.

The man of steady wisdom, having subdued them all (senses), becomes fixed in Me, the Supreme. His wisdom is well established whose sense are under control.

Thinking of sense-objects, man becomes attached thereto. From attachment arises longing and from longing anger is born.

From anger arises delusion; from delusion, loss of memory is caused. From loss of memory, the discriminative faculty is ruined and from the ruin of discrimination, he perishes.

For that which is born death is certain, and for the dead birth is certain. Therefore, grieve not over that which is unavoidable.

As in this body the embodied soul passes through childhood, youth and old age, in the same manner it goes from one body to another; therefore, the wise are never deluded regarding it…

As man casts off worn-out garments and puts on others which are new, similarly the embodied soul, casting off worn-out bodies, enters into others which are new.

***

Final Teaching

The Lord of Unlimited Power
dwells in the heart of all beings, Arjuna,
and by His magic power of illusion,
causes them to move about
like wooden dolls fixed on a machine.
Give your whole heart to that Supreme Lord,
seek refuge in Him alone;
by His Grace you will find perfect peace
and the abode of immortal life.

Abandon all hope of gain from this world
and take refuge in me alone;
I will wash away your every sin
and free you from every evil,
Never again will you grieve.

TRADITIONAL WISDOM

SHANKARACHARYA

This Atman (the inner Self) shines with its own light. Its power is infinite. It is beyond sense-knowledge. It is the source of all experience. He who knows the Atman is free from every kind of bondage. He is full of glory. He is the greatest of the great.

A Garland of Questions and Answers:

What is the first and most important duty for a man of right understanding?

To cut through the bonds of worldly desire.

To whom do the gods pay homage?
To one who is compassionate.

Who is dumb?
One who does not listen to good advice.

Who is dumb?
One who does not speak kind words when they are needed.

What is most to be deplored?
Miserliness in the wealthy.
Wherein, lies strength?
In patience.

Who profits from this life?
One who is humble.

***

SRI AUROBINDO

The Hour of God

There are moments when the Spirit moves among men and the breath of the Lord is abroad upon the waters of our being; there are others when it retires and men are left to act in the strength or the weakness of their own egoism. The first are periods when even a little effort produces great results and changes destiny; the second are spaces of time when much labour goes in to the making of a little result. It is true that the latter may prepare the former, may be the little smoke of sacrifice going up to heaven which calls down the rain of God's bounty.

Unhappy is the man or the nation which, when the divine moment arrives, is found sleeping or unprepared to use it, because the lamp has not been kept trimmed for the welcome and the ears are sealed to the call. But thrice woe to them who are strong and ready, yet waste the force or misuse the moment; for them is irreparable loss or a great destruction.

In the hour of God, cleanse thy soul of all self-deceit and hypocrisy, and vain self-flattering that thou mayst look straight into thy spirit and hear that which summons it. All insincerity of nature, once thy defence against thy eye of the Master and the light of the ideal, becomes now a gap in thy armour and invites the blow. Even if thou conquer for the moment, it is the worse for thee, for the blow shall come afterwards and cast thee down in the midst of thy triumph. But being pure, cast aside all fear; for the hour is often terrible, a fire and a whirlwind and a tempest, a treading of the winepress of the wrath of God; but he who can stand up in it on the truth of his purpose is he who shall stand; even though he fall, he shall rise again; even though he seems to pass on the wings of the wind, he shall return. Nor let worldly prudence whisper too closely in the ear; for it is the hour of the unexpected.

***

SRI RAMAKRISHNA

The magnetic needle always points towards the north, and hence it is that the sailing vessel does not lose her course. So long as the heart of man is directed towards Gods, he cannot be lost in the ocean of worldliness.

A husband and wife renounced the world and jointly undertook a pilgrimage to various religious shrines. Once, as they were walking on a road, the husband, being a little ahead of the wife, saw a piece of diamond on the road. Immediately he scratched the ground to hide the diamond, thinking that, if his wife saw it, she might perchance be moved by avarice and thus lose the merit of her renunciation. While he was thus busy, the wife came up and asked him what he was doing. In an apologetic tone he gave her an evasive reply. She noticed the diamond, however, and reading his thoughts, asked him 'Why have you left the world, if you still feel the difference between the diamond and the dust?'

So long as one does not become simple like a child, one does not get divine illumination. Forget all the worldly knowledge that thou hast acquired and become as ignorant as a child, and then will thou get the divine wisdom.

***

SRI RAMANA MAHARISHI

Brahmaloka cannot be gained so long as there is any desire left in the person. Desirelessness alone will confer the *loka* on him. His desirelessness signifies the absence of the incentive of rebirth.

Will-power should be understood to be the strength of mind which makes it capable of meeting success or failure with equanimity…Success develops arrogance and the man's spiritual progress is thus arrested. Failure on the other hand is beneficial, in as much as it opens the eyes of the man to his limitations and prepares him to surrender himself. Self-surrender is synonymous with eternal happiness. Therefore, one should try to gain the equipoise of mind under all circumstances. That is will-power.

***

SWAMI RAMDAS

Men of wisdom exhort us: 'Do not cry for the perishable.' 'Weep not for the dead.' Stand firmly fixed in the consciousness of your immortal Existence and see as an unperturbed witness, the passing vicissitudes of life, just as you witness the clouds that pass before your gaze. Let us watch the divine play on the world stage. People appear on it and disappear from it. The world is a passing show. We are the sun of Truth and the world a flitting panorama like the clouds. Whatever has name and form must change and vanish. It is only that immortal Truth, Spirit, or God, that nameless, formless, birthless and deathless Reality—with which we are one—that never changes and ever exists.

Just as a flower gives out its fragrance to whomsoever approaches or uses it, so love from within us radiates towards everybody and manifests as spontaneous service....When we feed, clothe, and attend on anybody, we feel like doing all these things to our own body, for which we do not expect any return or praise or commendation, because all bodies are our own; for, we as the all-pervading Atman or Spirit reside in all bodies.

***

SWAMI BRAHMANANDA

If you wish to work properly, you should never lose sight of two great principles: first, a profound respect for the work undertaken, and second, a complete indifference to its fruits.

Thus only can you work with the proper attitude. This is called the secret of Karma-Yoga. And you can overcome all aversion for a piece of work, if you but consider it as belonging to God.

***

SRIMAD BHAGAVATAM

All duties, if accompanied by devotion to me, lead to the supreme good and to eternal liberation. Rare indeed is this human birth. The human body is like a boat, the first and foremost use of which is to carry us across the ocean of life and death to the shore of immortality. The Guru is the skilful helmsman: divine grace is the favourable wind. If with such means as these, man does not strive to cross the ocean of life and death, he is indeed spiritually dead.

***

YOGA-VASISTHA

The supreme Spirit, unlimited by time, space, of His own will and by the power of His omnipotence, takes upon Himself the limited forms of time and space. Know that the world, although appearing as substantial in it: it is a void, being merely an appearance created by the images and vagaries of the mind. Know the world to be an enhanced scene, presented by the magic of maya.

ALSO FROM SPEAKING TIGER

SHIVA

Lord of the Cosmic Dance

Karan Singh

> 'A carefully put together [selection of] philosophical reflections and artistic and poetic compositions about Shiva...The editor and publisher deserve our gratitude for the insightful selection and beautiful production.' —Purushottam Agrawal, *The Tribune*

Of all the gods in Hinduism, Shiva is the most fascinating and intriguing. He stands outside, even contradicts, human categories and conventions. He is the misfit who challenges distinctions between sacred and profane, rich and poor, right and wrong. He is at once the great yogi, the ascetic-turned-householder and the vagabond. He is, finally, Lord of the Cosmic Dance—the timeless dance of dissolution, creation and regeneration.

This anthology is an attempt to explore and understand the diverse and enigmatic forms of this many-faceted god, through the thought and meditations of some of the finest poets, academics, scholars and devotees, across time and place—among them, Lal Ded, Mahadeviakka, Swami Vivekananda, Aldous Huxley, Kalidasa, Sri Aurobindo, Basavanna, Adi Shankaracharya, Acharya Abhinavagupta, Allama Prabhu, Ananda Coomaraswamy, Nazeer Akbarabadi, Namita Gokhale, Devdutt Pattanaik, Stella Kramrisch, Alka Pande, Wendy Doniger and Nilima Chitgopekar.

Whether you are a believer, an agnostic or on the fence, this superb collection, edited by Karan Singh—one of the most respected authorities on India's varied traditions and philosophies—will draw you deep into the mystery and wonder that is Shiva.